ELIZABETH TAYLOR

JOHN B.
ALLAN

BLACKBIRD BOOKS
NEW YORK • LOS ANGELES

A Blackbird Classic, July 2011

Manufactured in the United States of America.

Cataloging-in-Publication Data

Allan, John B.
Elizabeth Taylor / John B. Allan.
p. cm.
1. Taylor, Elizabeth, 1932-2011. 2. Motion picture actors and actresses—United States—Biography. I. Title.
PN2287.T18 A68 2011 927.92 2011933113

Blackbird Books
www.bbirdbooks.com
email us at editor@bbirdbooks.com

ISBN 978-1-61053-032-3

First Blackbird Edition

10 9 8 7 6 5 4 3 2 1

ELIZABETH
TAYLOR

THE DORCHESTER HOTEL, London, England. March 4, 1961. A suite—series of suites, actually—costing a reported $840 a week. Five days ago, the woman who lives here celebrated her twenty-ninth birthday. In a sense, she had come home, for she had been born here in London on February 27, 1932, though she had lived most of her life half a world away, in a Toyland on the shore of the Pacific.

Her name is Elizabeth Taylor. With her lives her fourth husband, Eddie Fisher, a popular singer who was boosted to the big time by Eddie Cantor. There are also the reminders of husband number three, Mike Todd—a daughter named Liza, a $92,000 engagement ring, half of a million-dollar business. And the reminders of husband number two, Michael Wilding—two sons, Michael and Christopher. There are no tangible reminders of Nick Hilton, husband number one.

At four o'clock in the morning, on Saturday the fourth of March, Eddie Fisher was on the telephone, making a hurried and desperate call to Dr. Carl Heinz Goldman, one of the many physicians who had nursed Elizabeth Taylor through the many illnesses of her lifetime, some real and some—according to insurance companies—not so real.

There was no question about this one, not the way Fisher described it to Dr. Goldman over the phone. She was having trouble breathing—she didn't seem able to get any air. She was beginning to show the effects of lack of oxygen.

Dr. Goldman hurried over. Within forty-five minutes, there was an oxygen tent in the hotel room, and soon the doctor was saying that she had only one or two hours left to live.

Other physicians were being called. They remembered her; they had been called four months earlier, in November of 1960, when Elizabeth Taylor had been suffering from a mysterious ailment that had turned out to be meningism, an unimportant children's disease, complicated by abscessed teeth. Doctors had also been called in December of 1959, when she had developed a somewhat more serious—though ultimately less expensive—case of pneumonia.

It was pneumonia this time, too, but a tougher breed. Staphylococcus pneumonia, the result of a bug that had grown resistant to most of the drugs used in the cure of pneumonia victims.

The odds were incredibly against her lasting the day. The doctors decided to take a long chance, and risked moving her to the London Clinic, the plush private hospital she had already spent so much time in for previous ailments. If she survived the trip—which seemed doubtful—she would have a better chance, with the equipment available to help her in the hospital.

At the clinic, Dr, Terence Cawthorne was getting ready to perform an emergency operation, should she manage to stay alive on the trip through the London streets from hotel to hospital. The planned operation was a tracheotomy, in which a slit opening is made in the windpipe and a tube inserted, to enable the patient to get more air.

She had a temperature of 103 degrees. Her right lung was severely congested. She was getting practically no air at all. She fluctuated at the edge of consciousness.

She was carried out and placed in the waiting ambulance. Eddie Fisher rode with her. No one seriously expected her to make it; they were merely taking the only chance left.

They drove her across London, her birthplace. It looked as though she had come home to die.

She had been away a long time and had lived a full—if not always happy—life. If London was where it was to end, that Toyland on the Pacific shore was where it had actually begun. . . .

BOOK I

In The Beginning

1

IT WAS A FAMILIAR SIGHT at the MGM studio in those days; the fierce, ambitious mother and the beribboned young daughter, welded together hand-to-hand, pushing their way into the studio in search of a magic screen test, with the name of one "contact" as a battering ram. If they were any different from the normal run of mother-daughter gate-crashers, it was in the fact that Mrs. Sara Sothern Taylor and her eight-year-old daughter, Elizabeth Taylor, both looked a lot healthier and a lot less insistent than their competition.

And at that time, the fall of 1940, the competition was rough. Shirley Temple had started it all with *Little Miss Marker,* six years before, her career proving conclusively that there was no box-office hype in the world greater than a little girl who could sing and dance. This was the era of the MGM musical—*Flying Down to Rio, Top Hat, Swing Time, Stand Up and Cheer,* and *Follow the Fleet* had already rolled off the MGM production line, and Gene Kelly's first film, *For Me and My*

Gal, would go before the cameras the following year—and a musical just wasn't a musical without a cute little child star. Tots of the Shirley Temple mold were all over Hollywood. Some few—notably Deanna Durbin, who had just been pirated from MGM by Universal Studios, and Gloria Jean, currently satirizing herself with the help of W. C. Fields in *Never Give a Sucker an Even Break*—had made the grade, but all the rest of the unfortunate tykes were still being hauled around town, from office to office, by their eager brittle-mannered mothers.

By now, six full years after *Little Miss Marker,* rumpled blond hair a la Temple was no longer absolutely necessary—Margaret O'Brien would be appearing in her first film, *Babes in Arms,* in less than a year—and so Mrs. Taylor left her daughter's black hair its original color. She had decided that Elizabeth would make the grade just as she was, without tampering with Nature's gifts.

Mrs. Sara Sothern Taylor was a shrewd, intensely farseeing mother who knew just what she wanted for her daughter. She was fully aware of Elizabeth's latent talents and was determined to find a niche in Hollywood for her daughter as so many youngsters had done before her. For ten years she guided Elizabeth's career with an unflagging energy, taking her wherever she felt there was a chance of winning an acting role in a current film.

Before her marriage, Mrs. Taylor had herself appeared on the stage under the name of Sara Sothern. She had come out of Midwest stock companies to play a supporting role in *The Fool,* both on Broadway and in the later London production. Returning to New York, she made the rounds fruitlessly for three years before appearing briefly in *The Little Spitfire.*

When, shortly after that show had closed, Francis Taylor—then a young man employed as an overseas representative by his art dealer uncle, Howard Young—proposed marriage, Sara Sothern accepted. Her theatrical career had been disappointingly slow and sporadic.

It was only natural that, given the opportunity, Mrs. Taylor would want to relive her career—to far greater triumphs than she had ever personally known—vicariously through her children. She tried with her son Howard first, he being two years older than his sister, but Howard absolutely refused to have anything to do with motion pictures. Mrs. Taylor was tenacious, but so was Howard, and he outlasted her, once going so far as to give himself a home haircut to avoid a screen test that his mother had set up for him.

With her daughter, Mrs. Taylor was much more successful. If she looked less adamant and bold than the general run of mothers beating at the studio gates, she was nevertheless far more enterprising than most of them. She planned her assault with care.

Of course, Mrs. Taylor did have one strong advantage over most of her competition: money. Her husband, Francis, was an art dealer, and did well at it, well enough to enable the family to take a house at Pacific Palisades, where Elizabeth Taylor could get to know the children of Darryl F. Zanuck and Norma Shearer. Her mother also enrolled her in a dancing class where she would be in contact with John Considine's daughter and with the two granddaughters of Louis B. Mayer.

Contacts, contacts, contacts, these are the ingredients of the Hollywood formula for the royal road to stardom. The children get to know one another, and then they meet each other's mummies, and then eventually some mummie says to her studio executive husband, "That Taylor child, now . . ."

However, before these proximity plans brought any results, a nibble came from another direction. This was the result of a temporary art gallery set up by Francis Taylor to display the paintings he had managed to evacuate from England early in World War II. Among these paintings were a number of Augustus Johns, and among the chief admirers of the work of Augustus Johns was a young lady named Andrea Berens. Miss Berens was engaged to marry J. Cheever Cowdin, at that time chairman of Universal Studios.

Mrs. Taylor demonstrated her daughter for Andrea Berens at the gallery one afternoon, and Miss Berens responded beautifully, saying, "I would like Cheever to see Elizabeth."

"Bring him out to the house on Sunday," Mrs. Taylor promptly suggested and, by way of further inducement, slyly added, "We have some more Augustus Johns paintings there."

No sooner said than done. Cowdin and Miss Berens arrived on Sunday. Mrs. Taylor, as soon as possible, bore Miss Berens away with her to look at the paintings, saying to her daughter on the way out, "Now, you show Mr. Cowdin how you can sing and act, dear."

It should be emphasized that, aside from money, proximity and contacts, Mrs. Taylor had one additional advantage over her competition, and this one, in the long run, made all the difference: her daughter had *talent*.

Elizabeth Taylor was a natural performer, delighted to have an audience, any audience at all. At the same tune, she was never a precocious brat, never a self-centered little egotist demanding attention and applause raucously and incessantly. Hers was a far healthier motivation—the simple desire to see that the people around her were at all times happy and entertained.

At the end of the afternoon, Cowdin suggested to Mrs. Taylor that she bring her daughter out to the Universal lot "sometime" for a screen test, and Mrs. Taylor said she thought that would be fine. However, Cowdin volunteered no specific date for this screen test, and Mrs. Taylor had too much sense ever to act the role of the shrill, pushy mother. And so the affair was left, for that afternoon, at that indefinite stage. Elizabeth Taylor would have a screen test sometime in the relatively near future. There was no reason to rush.

Nevertheless, Mrs. Taylor wasn't about to rest on her laurels. The next afternoon, Monday, when she brought her daughter to the dance class on La Cienega, she saw that Carmen Considine, the wife of John Considine, then a producer at MGM was also there. Elizabeth Taylor gave an impromptu songfest, and Mrs. Considine was suitably impressed. At the age of eight, Elizabeth Taylor had a strong, clear, melodic voice, and a fine sense of rhythm and tone.

Mrs. Considine talked with Mrs. Taylor about bringing her daughter to the MGM studio to meet John Considine.

"I'd love to," said Mrs. Taylor, "but I've already promised to bring Elizabeth over to Universal. Cheever Cowdin told me to bring her over for a screen test."

"Don't sign with him," said Carmen immediately. "Promise me that. Don't sign with him or with anyone else, at least not until John's had a chance to see Elizabeth and hear her sing."

Mrs. Taylor was only too glad to promise.

The next day, Tuesday, Mrs. Considine brought this mother and daughter—both of them, each in her own way, far more talented than any other mother-daughter combination then storming the gates—to her husband's office at MGM.

John Considine was interested at once, but the interview hit an early snag. It was nearly five-thirty in the afternoon when they arrived at the studio, and there wasn't a piano player left on the lot. Not one to give up her opportunities so readily, Mrs. Taylor herself sat down at the piano and, one-fingered, played C-E-G-C right up the keyboard, with Elizabeth Taylor singing on and around the notes, making up her own words as she went along.

Considine was impressed sufficiently to bring the girl—and her mother—directly to the office of Louis B. Mayer. Mayer looked at the eight-year-old girl, listened to her sing, and said, "Sign her up. What are you waiting for?" He then left the studio for the day.

And at that point, Mrs. Taylor balked. MGM was offering a seven-year contract at one hundred dollars a week, and it wasn't enough. Not that Mrs. Taylor exactly *said* that it wasn't enough. What she actually *said* was, "Well, we did promise Cheever Cowdin over at Universal that *he* could have a screen test of Elizabeth."

It was a good try. MGM had just lost Deanna Durbin to Universal. If they were interested enough in Elizabeth Taylor to want to prevent the same thing from happening with her, then they could talk in terms a lot better than a hundred dollars a week.

Regrettably, they didn't. MGM was big, the number of players it held under contract was already huge, and the number of mother-daughter combinations still out in the waiting room was undiminished. A hundred dollars a week was a hundred dollars a week, and that was all MGM was prepared to offer, and Mrs. Taylor could take it or leave it. She left it. She played her hand the only way she could. She took her daughter home unsigned, and the next morning she phoned Cheever Cowdin at Universal.

It seemed as though luck was running against Mrs. Taylor just then, for Cheever Cowdin wasn't in town. He had gone to New York, three thousand miles away. And yet *now* was the moment for Mrs. Taylor to strike, before MGM had a chance to cool, to forget that they had wanted Elizabeth Taylor. If she could get a screen test in the works at Universal, and let the news drift back to MGM, it just might make them come through with a better offer.

As with the piano incident in John Considine's office, Mrs. Taylor now once again demonstrated her flair for bulling through unexpected obstacles in her path—in a ladylike sort of way. She phoned Cowdin long distance, in New York, and told him about the MGM offer.

Cowdin had been impressed by Elizabeth Taylor that Sunday afternoon at the Taylor house, as well he might have been. Also, Universal was a quite frankly smaller upstart studio trying to grab some of the MGM lion's share of the motion picture market, and as a result was inevitably interested in *any* performer who had been offered a contract by MGM.

Accordingly, Cowdin made a fast decision. When Mrs. Taylor, in her coast-to-coast phone call to him, told him of

MGM's offer of a contract, he said, "How much did they offer?"

"One hundred dollars a week," she told him. "If MGM wants her," said Cowdin, "I want her. I'll double their offer. I'll telephone our studio tomorrow and tell them to give her a contract at *two* hundred a week." Mrs. Taylor accepted at once.

And here was a fantastic situation. Two major motion picture studios were offering long-term contracts for Elizabeth Taylor, and *neither studio had given her a screen test.* Nor had any official of either studio ever seen her in an actual performance, on the stage or in a motion picture or anywhere else. And yet two major studios wanted her.

Even at the age of eight, Elizabeth Taylor's brilliant potential was obvious. For it is an ever-startling fact that Elizabeth Taylor is not only one of the most beautiful women alive today, she is also one of our most accomplished actresses, combining a strong natural aptitude with years of study of her craft.

Her potential was sufficiently obvious to the heads of two major studios—Louis B. Mayer of MGM and J. Cheever Cowdin of Universal—to make both of them, personally, offer her contracts without a preliminary screen test.

Although Mrs. Taylor's decision to accept the offer of Universal Studios was motivated by a desire to do what she thought was best for her daughter, circumstances were later to prove that she had made a mistake—a mistake that would temporarily stall Elizabeth's career.

Mrs. Taylor had to ignore a number of facts in order to sign with Universal. She had to ignore MGM's greater size and greater potential as a star builder. She had to ignore the fact that Elizabeth Taylor herself disliked Universal and had said of MGM, "I know it's right for me to be here. I *know* it's right."

And, possibly most important of all, she had to ignore the fact that Dan Kelly, then casting director at Universal, was completely unimpressed by Elizabeth Taylor and once went so far as to say, "The kid has nothing. Her eyes are too old; she doesn't have the face of a kid."

Mrs. Taylor was a self-confident woman, a woman of strong convictions and unswerving loyalties. Although she was aware of the basic differences between the two studios, she felt that the move to Universal was the right one at the time. For that reason, the contract with Universal was signed that very same day, for seven years with yearly options, at two hundred dollars a week.

A number of years later, Mrs. Taylor gave her reason for having signed with Universal rather than MGM: "As it was a *smaller* studio, we thought it would be better for Elizabeth."

2

THE JOB OF A CASTING DIRECTOR is simply explained: He casts motion pictures.

Actually, there's a bit more to it than that. The major roles in a motion picture are usually cast by the man who will direct the shooting of the film, unless the producer is stronger-willed (David O. Selznick, for example) than the director. Supporting and minor roles are left to the casting director, who chooses this part of the cast from among the contract players.

Aside from the obvious requirement that the casting director choose actors who suit the parts reasonably well, there are a number of other requirements for him to keep in mind. It is a bad move, for instance, to give an actor a smaller role than the one he had in his most recently completed picture. It is a good move to give as many roles as possible to an actor who is getting extra push from the publicity department. And so on.

And, last but not least, the casting director makes his choices on the basis of what *he* thinks of the individual actors and actresses, *as performers*. If an actor impresses the studio's casting director, he will do well. If an actor gets himself disliked—*as a performer*—by the casting director, he is doomed, at least at that studio, and it doesn't matter how well he did on his screen test or how pleased the studio brass were to get him under contract. His fate lies in the hands of the casting director.

Elizabeth Taylor, at the age of eight, was under contract to Universal Studios. Dan Kelly was casting director there, and he thought Elizabeth Taylor was "nothing." He demonstrated this opinion in the one and only film in which he gave her a part.

It is generally believed that Elizabeth Taylor's first motion picture was *Lassie Come Home*, followed by the film which established her reputation as a child star, *National Velvet*. Most decidedly, the general belief is wrong. Both of these films were made at MGM, where Elizabeth Taylor had wanted to be signed in the first place, and where, eventually, she did come under contract. But before going to MGM, she spent a full year at Universal, where Dan Kelly finally cast her in one motion picture.

The film was entitled *Man or Mouse*—one of the least memorable motion pictures of our time. It starred Alfalfa Sweetzer, boy comic, and young Elizabeth Taylor had a small role as a brat who sang a duet with him. Alfalfa Sweetzer, by the way, had but one claim to fame—an unerring ability to sing off key.

Publicity releases on Elizabeth Taylor never mention *Man or Mouse*, and it's understandable. It was probably the only picture she ever made about which she could justifiably feel ashamed, though she could hardly be held responsible, either for the quality of the picture as a whole or for the circumstance of her participation in it.

Universal Studios did more for Elizabeth Taylor than cast her in the one motion picture she'd rather not talk about. It aided her career in a more telling manner as well. The studio forced her to take a singing lesson every weekday, with a teacher who apparently had a grudge against music or, at least, a grudge against Elizabeth Taylor.

In a magazine article, a number of years later, Mrs. Sara Sothern Taylor described what had been done to her daughter's voice in this manner: "By this time Elizabeth's voice had changed completely. It was little and thin. The year she was at Universal they had made her take a singing lesson every day. They wouldn't let her sing out as she had always done. They made her keep her voice *down* and *little*. They took all the *joy* out of her singing, and there was nothing much left." (Ladies Home Journal, March 1954)

It is probable that in the process of growing up Elizabeth Taylor's voice would have changed to some extent anyway. However, it seems likely that a careful and diligent teacher could have minimized the bad effects of this change, and that the brand of teaching Elizabeth Taylor *did* get served only to increase the bad effects of the change.

At any rate, having cast Elizabeth Taylor in one movie and having additionally helped to remove her singing voice, Universal Studios then simply paid out its contracted two hundred dollars a week until the first year was finished, and then did not pick up the option.

If at least her daughter's voice had still been good, Mrs. Taylor could then, with no hurt to her pride, have returned to MGM and signed a contract there. But not even that avenue was open.

Thus, without having had a full chance to exhibit her talents Elizabeth Taylor's career came to an abortive end when she was only nine years of age. The record: One motion picture, best forgotten. One singing voice, gone forever.

Mrs. Taylor, for the first time in her daughter's career, was at a loss. Elizabeth Taylor, who only a year before had been urgently wanted by two motion picture studios, was now definitely *not* wanted by either. And Howard still refused to have anything to do with the motion picture industry. It was a sorry situation all around.

In desperation, Mrs. Taylor dragged her daughter off to see Hedda Hopper. She had a letter of introduction to Miss Hopper from a mutual friend in England. Miss Hopper sat still long enough for Elizabeth Taylor to sing *Blue Danube*—her mother's choice—and then, in a statement startlingly mild for the often irascible Miss Hopper, said, "Frankly, I don't think Elizabeth's future lies in her singing."

For a number of months, it looked as though Elizabeth Taylor's future didn't lie anywhere within the entertainment field. But then, a few months after Pearl Harbor, the ever-present Mrs. Taylor heard that MGM was casting a film titled *Lassie Come Home,* and that they were having difficulty finding someone for the part of a young English girl.

Contacts, contacts. Mrs. Taylor searched for someone to serve as a contact with the casting powers concerned with *Lassie Come Home,* and soon she learned that the picture's producer, Sam Marx, lived in the neighborhood, on the street behind the Taylor house. She also learned that Sam Marx was an air-raid warden.

Mrs. Taylor sent her husband out with a tin helmet on his head. Francis, too, was an air-raid warden, and Francis had been primed by his wife to talk Sam Marx into at least *looking* at his daughter. Francis, a quiet, mild and easygoing man, followed instructions to the letter.

Sam Marx was interested. In the first place, he *was* having trouble finding a girl for the part. In the second place, Elizabeth Taylor had spent the first seven years of her life in England, and the girl in the movie was supposed to be English. And, in the third place, Elizabeth Taylor had once been signed by Universal and had appeared in a movie on the Universal lot, and so was not totally without experience.

These three items were enough for Marx. He told Taylor to bring his daughter around to the studio the next day for a test.

It was *Mrs.* Taylor who came to the studio with Elizabeth Taylor the following day. Sam Marx later described that day thus:

"We had there five other girls whom we were considering. We practically had selected one, because I didn't expect much from Elizabeth. But the moment she entered there was a complete eclipse of all the others. She was stunning, dazzling. Her voice was charming, and she had no self-consciousness whatsoever. We gave her a test, and when we looked at it the next day, we knew we had a find."

And so, a year and a half late, Elizabeth Taylor's acting career actually started. She was ten years old.

3

LASSIE COME HOME was Elizabeth Taylor's first real introduction to the American motion picture audience, and their first real introduction to her. Both sides had successfully forgotten *Man or Mouse.*

Although *Lassie Come Home* didn't establish her as a solid box-office favorite and potential star—it took the role of "Velvet" in the movie *National Velvet* to do that—this first film did give her a reputation sufficiently good for Twentieth Century-Fox to request her for a loan-out to appear in *Jane Eyre,* and for her to return to MGM to appear opposite Roddy McDowall in *White Cliffs of Dover.*

It was in *Lassie Come Home* that Elizabeth Taylor first rode horseback before a motion picture camera, and her ease and skill as a rider were a strong recommendation when it came time to cast the role of the young girl in *National Velvet.*

Actually, few children had better preparation for the role. At the age of ten, Elizabeth Taylor had been an accomplished equestrienne for half her life, having been given a pony named Betty when she was only five years of age. And Betty gave her a rough introduction to the joys of riding.

It happened in May of 1957, when the Taylor family was living in England, in a country home called "Little Swallows" on the Victor Cazalet estate near Cranbrook, Kent, sixty miles from London. Cazalet was the donor of Betty. Though the pony was given to Elizabeth, it was her older brother, Howard, who took the first ride, and with Howard holding the reins Betty behaved beautifully. But when Elizabeth Taylor was lifted onto the pony's back behind Howard by her father, Betty threw her right back off again, and she landed in a patch of stinging nettles. She was burned from head to foot, but the Taylor governess grabbed handfuls of dock weed and rubbed the little girl's body with it until the swelling and stinging lessened.

Shaken but determined, the five-year-old girl walked the pony around the area for a while, talking to her, explaining to her that she was her new owner and that they were supposed to get along. When both the pony and the prospective rider had calmed down sufficiently, the new owner mounted once more and rode her pony with no trouble at all. Nor did she ever have trouble with Betty again.

Elizabeth Taylor's uncanny ability to tame animals has been demonstrated again and again. One unexpected bit of expert horsemanship on her part was filmed in the Lassie picture, though it didn't appear in the finished movie. The horse she was riding in one scene became frightened when he passed a light reflector. He shied away from the reflector and reared, forelegs pawing the air, and then tried to climb over a wall. She managed to rein the frightened animal, soothe him, and continue to ride him to the spot where, if the scene had continued on to the end as planned, she was to have dismounted, opened a gate, and exchanged some dialogue with Nigel Bruce, one of the featured players in the film. Having calmed the frightened horse, she did just that, following through to the end of the scene anyway.

Elizabeth Taylor's affinity and fondness for animals has remained a constant through her life. As of June, 1960, her household, aside from the human beings, included four dogs, two cats and a monkey. A reporter who went to interview her in 1949 listed her then-current pets: "There are one springer spaniel, one cocker, an English golden retriever, a black poodle, a white poodle, two cats, one squirrel, and one chipmunk at her home and two horses at a boarding stable."

Psychologists, both professional and amateur, basing their ideas on published newspaper and magazine stories and *not* on personal observation and study of their subject, have explained Elizabeth Taylor's love for animals in this way: As a child, she was very lonely. Her father was quiet and mild. Her mother was occupied with fostering Elizabeth's career and could not give her the attention she needed.

When she was very young, around three years of age, her governess discovered that the most effective punishment possible with this little girl was to "put her in Coventry," to not speak to her or pay any attention to her, to make believe one couldn't hear her and didn't see her and didn't know she existed.

Mrs. Taylor, seeing that the punishment was effective, allowed it to continue because she believed it was a form of discipline that would curb the child's behavior problems. After Elizabeth had started school the *only* way for her to communicate with her mother, once she had been put in

Coventry, was to write a note of apology and leave it on her mother's pillow. Mrs. Taylor still keeps and treasures these pathetic apologies, some carefully printed when her daughter was barely seven years of age.

It is true that Elizabeth Taylor's home life, as a child, was never particularly conducive to mental health. At the same time, she did have a two-years-older brother at home, with whom she got along uncommonly well, and she seems to have never, during her childhood, had too much trouble finding girl friends her own age. Nor is loneliness and natural affection always a prerequisite to a fondness for animals. It seems altogether possible that Elizabeth Taylor would have been fond of dogs, cats, monkeys and horses no matter what her childhood was like. After all, she has always demonstrated a deep capacity for appreciating the problems of others and has always shown a strong inner sensitivity.

Because of the horse-riding scene in *Lassie Come Home,* Elizabeth Taylor was sent by MGM to a riding instructor, a woman named Mrs. Leo Dupee. When Mrs. Dupee saw how quickly and how naturally her young charge took to riding, and the immediate sense of trust between her and her mount, she said, "Elizabeth, you must learn to jump. I have a feeling you'll be doing a lot of riding in pictures."

This early work with Mrs. Dupee, plus her performance in *Lassie Come Home,* made her a potential choice for the important role of the little girl in *National Velvet.* This was to be an important picture, from a financial standpoint, and the studio was casting it with the greatest of care.

Among the host of actresses already tested for the part, over a period of years, had been Margaret Sullavan and Katherine Hepburn. Any girl or woman with acting ability who could even remotely be made to resemble the child heroine of *National Velvet* was being tested.

This included Elizabeth Taylor. She did very well in her preliminary auditions for the part, which surprised no one, and was returned to Mrs. Dupee for further riding lessons.

It was also during the filming of *Lassie Come Home* that Elizabeth Taylor first demonstrated herself to be accident-prone. (Accidents and diseases have so hampered her working career through the years that today she is considered by insurance companies the worst insurance risk of any star in the motion picture industry.)

On the last day of filming, the same horse she had a week or two earlier calmed with such unexpected efficiency now accidentally stepped on her foot, injuring it severely. She had to be taken to the hospital, where the foot had swollen so badly her jodhpur boot had to be cut off.

Although this was her first serious accident, one of the diseases which was to plague her from time to time throughout her life had struck for the first time seven years before, in March of 1935, when she was barely three years of age. A simple sore throat developed into a serious and unusual complication—abscessed ears, which were extremely painful and which, in addition, had to be lanced over and over again. She couldn't lie down at all, but had to stay propped up in bed in a sitting position. Hot poultices had to be kept at all times on both ears, and she had a temperature of 103 degrees for three weeks.

Elizabeth Taylor's life has been a long grim jest played by a grotesque god. She has been given far more than the average woman, in terms of wealth, fame, talent, beauty and love, and yet there has been a brutal balancing of the books, for she has also suffered far more than the average woman, in terms of sickness, accident, viciously bad publicity, broken marriages and the death of loved ones. She has paid, it seems, for every good thing she has ever received, paid to the last single cent of physical and mental torment.

However, this leg injury was the only serious physical disability that was to strike her during the first section of her motion picture career. She came out of the hospital to audition for *National Velvet* and to be loaned out to Twentieth Century-Fox for *Jane Eyre.* Then, because she was a strong possibility for the part in *National Velvet,* she returned to her riding instructor, Mrs. Dupee, at the Dupee Stables, to learn how to jump hurdles on horseback.

The studio also hired Snowy Baker, the Australian polo player, to teach her steeplechasing, at the Riviera Country Club. At this time, though only eleven years of age, Elizabeth Taylor was busier than most adults. In addition to the time she spent in front of a camera every weekday and the three hours of school at the studio grammar school (required by California state law), she could be found for at least two hours a day, every day, riding either with Mrs. Dupee at the Dupee stables or with Snowy Baker at the Riviera Country Club.

It was at the Riviera Country Club, and during this period, that Elizabeth Taylor first saw King Charles, the horse she would later talk the studio into using as The Pi in *National Velvet.*

She asked the King's owner, a Miss Charles, if she might be allowed to ride him, but Miss Charles told her that King (a grandson of Man O' War) was too high-spirited and temperamental, that she never allowed anyone but herself to ride him.

So Elizabeth Taylor simply sat and watched as King Charles' groom walked him till he was cool, then brushed him down and put him into his stable for the night. She noticed that the groom did not enter the stable to give King his hay dinner, but tossed it through an opening high in the wall between the stable and the hay bin.

When she asked him why he chose this roundabout method to get food to King, he explained that King never let anyone at all into the stable with him. If the groom—or anyone else—were to enter King's stable when he was in it, they would be kicked right back out again, along with some slats from the stable walls.

After King Charles had been fed, and the groom had locked the stable and gone off to have his own supper, Elizabeth Taylor wormed her way into the hay bin, and up the piled hay to the dinner slot, where she could see King in his stall. She spoke to him, quietly, until he got used to the idea of her *voice* being in the stall with him, and then she crawled through and dropped onto his back. He reacted, at first, as violently as she had been led to expect, but she simply flattened herself against his back, clung to him, and continued to talk quietly and reassuringly to him until he calmed down.

From then on, she spent half an hour or more with King Charles late every afternoon, until the inevitable afternoon when she was caught. It was King's owner, Miss Charles, who discovered the eleven-year-old girl perched atop King in his stall, and she was so startled she gave the girl permission to ride King Charles before she knew what she was doing.

Just before coming to the Riviera Country Club to be trained in the steeplechase by Snowy Baker, Elizabeth Taylor and her mother had met with Pandro Berman, the producer of *National Velvet.* Berman was sold on her for the movie, but there was one problem. She was much shorter than Mickey Rooney, who was to play Mi. Berman wanted to start actual filming in three months, but Elizabeth Taylor was three inches too short. He told her, "Well, Elizabeth, you're still too small. We want to start in three months, and you should be three inches taller."

"I'll grow, Mr. Berman," she promised. "I'll grow the three inches."

She did. Probably if she hadn't, Pandro Berman would have waited a month or two more. Nevertheless, she did grow to the requested height within the requested time, and shooting on the picture began.

King Charles, at Elizabeth Taylor's urgent request, was bought by the studio from Miss Charles, and appeared in *National Velvet* as The Pi. However, it was more or less a trade, since the studio executives, not as completely confident in her ability as a horsewoman as she was, exacted from her a promise that she would limit her riding to that done before the camera, at least until *National Velvet* was finished and in the can.

It took seven months to film *National Velvet,* and nearly every day of shooting resulted in someone being injured. Only three people in the cast who appeared on horseback managed to avoid injury and hospitalization. Two of these were jockeys from the steeplechase scene, and the third, surprisingly enough, was Elizabeth Taylor, virtually the only time in her life when the physical jinx hasn't struck her down.

Eventually *National Velvet* was finished. Having seen a sneak preview of the picture, Elizabeth Taylor was asked what she thought of it, and replied, "Wasn't The Pi wonderful? I knew he could do it!" She apparently meant the race which The Pi won in the movie—she was understandably rattled. When asked what she thought of her own performance in the film, she answered, "I've always *loved* Velvet!"

4

ELIZABETH TAYLOR is today twenty-nine years of age. For the last twenty-one of those years, she has lived in an artificial environment as cozy but as dangerous as a germ-free laboratory. Scientists have experimented with the physical effects of environment by raising animals in hermetically-sealed and guaranteed antiseptic cages, and then finally breaking the seal and exposing the animals to the normal world. The first passing germ knocks them over.

From the age of eight, Elizabeth Taylor has lived in a pastel-pink prison, where the bars are cloud-shaped but are bars nonetheless. The prison is sealed. There is only fantasy within. Reality is sprayed away at the studio gate.

Every once in a while, a bit of reality gets in. That can be hell.

This prison, in which the cells are padded with marshmallows and the strait jackets are made of gingerbread, was constructed with the willing help of a lot of people, and with no malicious intent at all. The film studios themselves furnished the capital for construction of these ivory ghettoes, and gave them their *raison d'être.*

The parents of the child stars, either through ambition for their youngsters, or through a vicarious self-fulfillment in the product of their loins, permitted this stultification and intellectual, emotional gelding of their children. California state law, with its frantic concern for the reputations and incomes of the children but not for their development as human beings, delineated the *form* of this child-hothouse. And finally the general public, in its demand for a pink-ribboned and palatable movie mythology, gave tacit approval to this monstrous edifice and heaped upon its inmates their temporary plaudits.

Most of these reality-immune children spent only a relatively short time in Fantasyville. They were loved as child stars, but once they reached the awkward teens, when voices were changing, bodies were growing gawkier and faces were no longer cute while not yet beautiful, they were out on their protected ears. Bobby Driscoll, Yvette Dugay, Gigi Perreau, Gloria Jean—there were a lot more, and these were perhaps the luckiest.

Then there were the few who lost the initial idolatry of their public but never *completely* lost their grip on the public fancy—Peggy Ann Garner, Donald O'Connor, Margaret O'Brien, Shirley Temple—still *of* the entertainment world to one degree or another, but no longer so completely buried *in* it as to suppose that nothing else exists in all the universe.

And finally, there are the ones who never left the ivory ghetto at all, and few are their number: Mickey Rooney, Judy Garland, Elizabeth Taylor. But the ivory ghetto was constructed for children, and in growing up (not maturing, simply *growing)* they have thrashed around and caused breaks in the seal, and reality keeps seeping in. Among these three there have been nearly a dozen marriages and at least one recorded suicide attempt.

And of the three, it is Elizabeth Taylor who has managed to retain most of the trappings of the ivory ghetto—she's more famous today than she was at twelve, and she's still working constantly, and she's the highest-paid actress in the world today.

What does the ghetto look like? And did Elizabeth Taylor *want* to enter it?

As to the second question, her mother says yes. "She loved making pictures, so that it was like play—not work. . . . *She* was the one who had wanted to be in pictures."

On the other hand, an old friend of the family was told by Mrs. Taylor: "It was almost impossible to believe—finding myself in the film capital with my children." She strove for seven years to get her son Howard into the movies—continued to try to push him into a film career time after time long after he had made it clear that he was uninterested—and didn't give up until, at the age of seventeen, Howard shaved his head to avoid a screen test his mother had set up for him with the assistance of Elizabeth Taylor's agent, Jules Goldstone.

It would seem, then, that the fact that Elizabeth Taylor was pliable enough to allow herself to be shoved into a motion picture career by her mother does not imply any particular desire for such a career on her part.

Her own statements on the subject have been oblique, but have implied the reverse. She admires and respects her brother Howard—now a marine artist at the Scripps

Institution of Oceanography—more than anyone else on earth, and has said of him, "I've always admired Howard for resisting becoming an actor and for making a career for himself in the work he likes best."

The work he likes best.

It seems obvious that Elizabeth Taylor was never given a chance to discover what work she might like best. Nor will she ever be able to find out. Her fame, her training and her continuing reliance on the ivory ghetto have all limited her to just the one occupation: movie star.

A more revealing statement was made by her in 1956: "The reason I suddenly became interested in acting in the past two years is that I finally got tired of all the garbage. In fifteen years, I've only made four pictures I really loved: *National Velvet, A Place in the Sun, The Last Time I Saw Paris* and *Giant.*"

She *suddenly became interested in acting* in 1954. Her mother maneuvered her into her first acting contract in 1940. Though she was resigned to the life from the outset, it took Elizabeth Taylor fourteen years to get interested in it!

George Stevens, who directed her in two of the four movies she loved from her first fourteen years of work—*A Place in the Sun* and *Giant*—has described a part of the ivory ghetto in this manner:

". . . she . . . had an artificial patriarchy imposed on her—the studio. It took the place of her own retiring father. The studio, like a domineering parent, was alternately stern and adoring. All day long, some official was telling her what to do and what not to do. She spent all of her pre-adolescent and adolescent days inside the walls of Metro-Goldwyn-Mayer. She worked on the set every morning and spent three hours in the MGM schoolroom every afternoon. She had no time to play, no contact with other children. Between takes, she was sent off to a vacant room somewhere to study."

Stevens also describes Mrs. Taylor's contribution to the ivory ghetto:

"Elizabeth was never allowed to speak for herself. When we had lunch in the studio commissary, Mrs. Taylor would preface most of her remarks with 'Elizabeth thinks' or 'Elizabeth says,' until I finally felt like shouting, 'Why don't you let Elizabeth say it herself?'"

Summing up, Stevens says:

"She was kept in a cocoon by her mother, by her studio, by the fact that she was the adored child who had had everything she wanted since she was eight years old."

Of course, she didn't *sleep* at the studio. She did go home at night. A friend of those days has described the home in this manner: "There were from six to twelve photographs of her in each room, sometimes posed alone, sometimes posed beside her mother."

Mrs. Taylor awoke her daughter in the morning, ate breakfast with her, drove her to the studio, kept in her sight at the studio all day long, drove her home again in the evening, chatted with her all evening, and at last, reluctantly, tucked her into bed. This was the daily regime. A magazine article four years ago stated: "At the dinner table, she (Mrs. Taylor) talked ceaselessly to Elizabeth and about her; Francis Taylor and Howard ate in silence."

It got bad enough for Howard to refuse pointblank every film career suggestion his mother ever made. It got bad enough for Francis Taylor to leave his wife temporarily.

Mrs. Taylor, in fact, wasn't content to share control of her daughter with the studio. In all of her early movies, Elizabeth Taylor had *two* directors; the one hired by the studio and her mother. The director hired by the studio told her what to do. Her mother sat unobtrusively in a corner and gave her constant hand signals in a prearranged code: hand on stomach meant voice too shrill, hand on heart meant not enough feeling, finger to cheek meant not enough smile, finger on neck meant overacting, finger to head meant not enough attention to the job, and so on and so on.

Years later a friend was to say of her: "She's grown up in a jungle that she's not out of yet. Most of the advice she's had came from self-interested people who, regardless of their affection for her, looked on her as a million-dollar property."

A perfect demonstration of what the friend had in mind concerns Elizabeth Taylor's education. When she graduated from the studio high school—with marks ranging from very good to very bad, depending on her interest in the subject—a friend of the family said to Mrs. Taylor, "Sara, this girl has a fine mind, and she wants to develop it. I think you ought to let her continue her studies at UCLA or some other college."

"Hmmph!" said Mrs. Taylor. "I bet all those girls going to UCLA wish they were Elizabeth Taylor."

BOOK II

Revolution in Toyland

5

CONTRAST AND CONTRADICTION have been the thematic undercurrents of Elizabeth Taylor's life. Before going to the studio that made a star of her, she spent a year at a studio that wasted her and threw her away. The first time didn't take; it required two tries.

This has been the hallmark of her life ever since. The first time doesn't take, not ever. Not even in stardom.

After *National Velvet,* Elizabeth Taylor was a star. The *first* time.

The problem was one of age. She was twelve when she made *National Velvet,* and twelve is just about the top limit of the child-star age range. The gawky, gangly early teens are fresh on the horizon. At thirteen or fourteen, when a girl actress is too old to be cute and too young to be sexy, there just aren't any possible movie roles that will help to maintain her popularity.

In this case, Elizabeth Taylor—and MGM—had the advantage of having already seen Shirley Temple go through this phase three years earlier. Miss Temple had attained fantastic popularity with such films as *Rebecca of Sunnybrook Farm,* in 1938, and MGM had tried to keep her popularity from waning during early adolescence by keeping her in the public eye, casting her steadily in films. This exposure of Miss Temple during the unlovely transitional years had just the reverse effect from that hoped for by the studio. Public adulation of her waned, and she was never able to recapture fully the popularity she had claimed as a child.

With Elizabeth Taylor, MGM tried a different method.

However, before the lean and lanky years set in, Elizabeth Taylor did make one more film. It was a surprising regression in casting, after the success of *National Velvet,* and it was to be her last motion picture for three years.

It was a war movie, about the Underground in one of the occupied European nations. The hero of the film was a collie named Bill, and the film itself was about as bad as that fact suggests. The title, for some unfathomable reason, was changed from its original *Hold High the Torch* through *Blue Sierra* to *The Courage of Lassie.* Lassie did not appear in the picture; only Bill.

Part of this film was shot on location near Lake Chelan in Washington State. In addition to the collie named Bill, there were any number of other animals integrally inserted in the plot of the film, all the charges of Curley Twyford, an animal trainer. Twyford and Elizabeth Taylor got along famously from the outset, as was to be expected, since they shared an affectionate interest in animals. It was from Twyford that she got Nibbles, the chipmunk that was to be her favorite pet for the next four years.

After *The Courage of Lassie* was completed, the three years of no movies began. But this doesn't mean that Elizabeth Taylor spent three years away from the studio. Far from it. She spent as much time as ever at the studio—all day long, five days a week—with one important difference: she was never before a camera.

It's hardly surprising that the products of this sort of environment come to physical maturity with a somewhat narrow and restricted view of reality. To most people, a motion picture studio is a studio where motion pictures are made. To Elizabeth Taylor, for the first three years of her teens, a motion picture studio was the place where she spent her days, attended school, met everyone she knew, gave interviews to pre-screened reporters, had her picture taken, ate her lunch and killed time. The studio was not a place where one went to work; the studio was the world.

Elizabeth Taylor's position in this world, for three years, was an eerie one. She was a movie star—who didn't make movies.

This was the studio's answer to the problem of the transitional years. The method tried with Shirley Temple had failed; here was a different solution. The studio realized that it could only harm a child star's popularity to show her to the public as she went gangling through her early teens. If they could manage to keep her *name* before the public, plus occasional carefully posed still photos, and age her gradually and gently in successive press releases, she just might be salvaged. Then, whenever the transition to ingenue was complete—at seventeen or sixteen or even, hopefully, fifteen—she could be put before the cameras again, with her luster undimmed, her public undisturbed, and her potential undiminished.

The most frequent way chosen by studio publicity departments to keep female stars before the public eye between pictures is to ballyhoo their marriages, their romances and their casual flings. Publicity departments can invent romances, if all else fails, and with the cooperation of a particularly ambitious couple a whole marriage can be engineered, thus ending heaven's monopoly in that regard.

This route, however, is rather effectively closed when the female star is thirteen or fourteen years of age. At least it was in 1946.

In three years, the publicity department managed—hampered as they were by the impossibility of bringing sex into the picture—to create four newsworthy items around Elizabeth Taylor to keep her before the public eye. And the four were good ones: She wrote a book. She sold a painting. She received a Ford convertible at the age of fourteen. She was given King Charles, the horse she rode in *National Velvet*, by the studio.

6

THE HORSE CAME FIRST. The studio gave it to her, with enough ballyhoo for a moon shot, on her thirteenth birthday. But if it was simply good publicity from the studio's viewpoint, it was an honestly welcomed gift from the viewpoint of Elizabeth Taylor.

This kind of thing has frequently caused cynicism among her fans, for it is unlikely but true that virtually everything engineered for her by her mother or by the studio has been something that she wanted anyway, with no ulterior motives. A part of this, of course, has been the natural passivity she's been struggling to overcome in the past few years. But in some instances she and her mentors desired the same things for quite different reasons.

It was undoubtedly passivity that led her into a motion picture career in the first place; she seems to have had no strong feelings one way or the other on the subject, which is not unusual for an eight-year-old. On the other hand, there is no question but that she was overjoyed when the studio gave her King Charles (named The Pi in *National Velvet),* nor is there any question but that her love of animals is genuine.

If there were any falseness in Elizabeth Taylor's fondness for animals, she would surely have given it up by now. In the first place, it would have seemed perfectly legitimate to her fans had she allowed this characteristic to fade away after she had left her latter teens. In the second place, a fraudulent affection for animals would be a bit difficult to maintain in a household already filled by three small children. And in the third place, its publicity value has long since dropped to nil.

When MGM gave her King Charles for her thirteenth birthday, therefore, it was to her a fine gift, in and of itself, and the publicity involved was incidental. To the studio, of course, it was the other way around. Yet, despite the difference of motive and reaction, the desires of Elizabeth Taylor and of MGM came down to a single result.

With the automobile, however, it was a different situation. Giving a young girl an automobile for her fourteenth birthday is ridiculous on the face of it—child star or no, she can't very well drive to work at that age—and a quiet apathy on the part of the child is certainly to be expected. There was no point in Elizabeth Taylor saying, "But I don't *want* a Ford convertible!" Nobody was asking her to do anything with it but stand beside it and smile for the photographers.

Neither of these gifts—a horse (the grandson of Man O' War) at thirteen, and a Ford convertible at fourteen—did Elizabeth Taylor any particular harm: after all, she could ride King Charles with no danger, and there was even less danger of her being given permission to drive the Ford. They both did her positive good, in fact, since both gifts—ballyhooed to the sky—helped to keep her name before the public during the dry years when she wasn't making any movies. The worst that can be said for these gifts is that they did their part in keeping Elizabeth Taylor safely oblivious of reality.

In reality, little girls of thirteen do *not* own horses who can trace their lineage to Man O' War. In reality, little girls of fourteen do *not* own Ford convertibles. In Toyland—otherwise known as the MGM studio—little girls own both.

In Toyland, little girls also write publishable books. The one Elizabeth Taylor wrote, at fourteen, was titled *Nibbles and Me,* and was a memoir, for juvenile consumption, of her relationship with the chipmunk given her by Curley Twyford. It was published by Duell in New York in 1946, paperbound for a dollar and clothbound for two dollars, with a Canadian edition published by Collins at a slightly higher price.

That Elizabeth Taylor actually did write the book herself there seems little doubt. That it was heavily edited—and probably by her mother—there seems less doubt. Consider this excerpt, which is not about Nibbles but which gives the publicity version of the King Charles birthday gift:

> The one thing in the world I wanted, and which I had always wanted from the day I first saw him, was King Charles (or The Pi, as he was called in National Velvet). I had finally talked mummie and daddy into letting me buy him, and every day for a week I had been going up to Mr. Thau's office, but he was off the lot and didn't come in. So the day before my birthday I was feeling so low because I didn't even know whether they would sell him to me or not, now that he was a big star, getting fan mail and all, and him costing such a lot of money. My heart was very heavy and I told Marjory Reeves, Mr. Thau's secretary, all about it. She said, "Don't worry, Elizabeth, you go home and I'll talk to Mr. Thau about it when he comes in."

> Marjory is so sweet and understanding and I knew it was in good hands. To make a long story short, the next day—the most wonderful birthday in all my life—Marjory called up and said, "Happy Birthday, Elizabeth, and Mr. Thau wants to speak to you."
>
> My heart stood still, and then as I heard what he had to say I screamed, "Jeepers." Mummie said I screamed "Jeepers" three times, and jumped straight up in the air each time. Just thinking about it now, and remembering, I still want to scream and jump, and I can still hear Mr. Thau saying, "Elizabeth, we're *giving* you King Charles for your birthday!"

This was the work of Elizabeth Taylor, at fourteen, for publication. The following was her work a year later, but not for publication. It refers to a bombed country church she saw in England in 1947, with only a fragment of wall left standing, that fragment containing a stained-glass window. It was quoted by her mother in *The Ladies Home Journal* early in 1954:

WATCHING THERE

Far down that twisting turning road
A country church is resting.
Its tired bones have fallen there,
Amongst the buried dead.
Its steeple which had held his head so high,
Is buried there, beneath his own dear cross.
Its stained-glass windows have had to take their flight.
All but one—a lonely figure watching there,
From her tattered glass.
For many years, through sun and rain, life and death,
She has kept her holy vigil.
And now for many more, through peace
And then through war,
She will hold her holy wake.
And now the little church is resting,
Laid down his head to sleep,
For watching and guarding over him is a figure,
Standing in a window stained with blood,

But with the golden rays of God's great love
Shining through her tattered image,
As they, together, keep their holy vigil.

As with King Charles and the Ford convertible, the publication of *Nibbles and Me* did Elizabeth Taylor no great harm. As with the other two, it did her good, keeping her in the public eye. And the book did her more good than that, for it made her money. The saccharine sort of public self-view it recommended was perhaps somewhat unrealistic, and the fact that it was the one item chosen among her writings for publication might have implied to her a somewhat distorted sense of values, but in comparison with the rest of her life in Toyland during this period these points are minor indeed.

The fourth newsworthy item from these inactive years was Elizabeth Taylor's sale of a watercolor landscape to a greeting card company. The painting was perfectly adequate greeting card art.

Her second serious accident, requiring hospitalization, also occurred during the transitional years. She—and her ever-present mother—were lunching together in the studio commissary. Suddenly, realizing that she was late for her singing lesson—MGM was using these inactive years in a futile attempt to bring back the singing voice that had been lost a few years before—she left the also ever-present Nibbles with her mother and ran for the commissary door. The heel of her shoe stubbed in a seam of the linoleum floor, and she fell forward with a scream of pain. When her mother reached her, she was crying, "I heard the bone break, I heard it break!"

The studio ambulance rushed her to the studio hospital—even a serious accident couldn't tear Elizabeth Taylor away from this self-contained world—where it was discovered that her foot was broken in three places. A cast was put on her foot, up to the knee, and she spent the next few days in the hospital. After she got out of the hospital, she spent three weeks on crutches, with her foot still in the cast, and a few more days dependent on the crutches after the cast had been taken off.

The reality of pain was beginning to creep into Toyland.

7

ELIZABETH TAYLOR was once asked how she'd liked those three and a half years of inactivity between *Courage of Lassie,* made when she was twelve, and *Cynthia,* her next film, shot when she was sixteen. Her answer was a miracle of brevity:

"I hated it."

And she wasn't the only one. Her mother was also anxious to see the time of inactivity come to an end. She did everything she could think of to hurry the aging process; after years of well-publicized childhood, Elizabeth Taylor found herself suddenly being hustled along toward physical maturity by her mother, while at the same time Mrs. Taylor required just as much obedience and dependence, on the emotional and intellectual levels, as ever. Contradiction was still the main motif of her life.

Mrs. Taylor decided that a part of her daughter's problem, insofar as juvenility was concerned, was her tomboyish concern for animals, and most particularly for horses, an interest that reflected itself not only in the completely unglamorous clothing she wore—rough riding clothes, shirttails flying—but even in the appointments of her bedroom. Two wooden sawhorses were along one wall, with saddles draped over them. Another saddle could usually be found on her dressing table stool, yet another one on her desk, and one or two more scattered around on the floor. Bridles were draped over the wall light brackets, and currycombs and other paraphernalia of the stable were placed helter-skelter around the room.

Mrs. Taylor changed all that. Rather than risk a revolution, she held off making the change until she could "surprise" her daughter with it, and then she made the change complete. Saddles and bridles and all the other tack room gear were removed from the bedroom. The gray carpet was dyed Du Barry red. A Queen Anne walnut settee was added, matching the desk. Bedspread, curtains, draperies and upholstery were all of white and pink and red, and two Epstein watercolors of roses were placed on the walls. In this atmosphere, a tomboy could hardly help but begin to think feminine.

Speaking of this change a number of years later, Mrs. Taylor said, "Looking back on it, I realize that it was an invasion of her privacy suddenly to remove all her treasures—her saddles, bridles, and so on. There was so little left of her room as *she* liked it; it was more her room the way *I* liked it."

Once the bedroom had been changed, Mrs. Taylor started a neatness campaign to keep her daughter from converting the room into something comfortable. Sitting on the bed was prohibited, clothing had to be hung up and put away, dresser drawers had to be inspection-perfect. Of this campaign, she was later to say, "I wish I had never worried her over such trifles. After all, what good did it do?"

The hurry-up-and-be-a-woman campaign had other aspects as well. Elizabeth Taylor developed a mature body at fourteen, and her mother chose her clothing with an eye to advertising this fact. Wide, tightly-drawn belts emphasized her narrow waist, while tight skirts and peasant blouses emphasized her abundance in other areas. Lipstick, nail polish, eye make-up, plucked eyebrows and more mature hairdos made their contributions as well.

The maturing process, on the emotional level, was also hastened, in two ways. First, there was the separation of her parents when she was fifteen years old. The separation only lasted a few months, during which time Elizabeth Taylor lived with her mother at a beach club. Secondly, she went through two years of humiliation and frustration as a dateless teenager with parents who tried all the wrong ways to find her a date.

To begin with, not just any boy was *allowed* to date Elizabeth. Her mother had to approve all applicants, and her standards were rigid. Secondly, any date she might have could not be *only* a date; it would also have to be— the studio and Mrs. Taylor agreed on this, and Elizabeth Taylor wasn't consulted—an opportunity for publicity.

As a result, there just weren't any applicants. When Elizabeth Taylor went to a dance or canteen with her brother Howard, or with Anne Westmore—her girlhood chum—the boys would stand around and stare at the movie star, but none of them could ever get his courage up and go ask her for a dance or—bravery of braveries!— even for a date.

Of course, there was one intimidating factor aside from the fact that Elizabeth Taylor was a well-known movie star: Her mother was usually hovering in the background, and that kind of thing will keep teenage boys away in hordes. When Melvina McEldowney of the MGM publicity department invited her daughter Gay's entire high school class to her house for a party—specifically so Elizabeth Taylor could come and perhaps meet some boys—only one party-goer arrived with a mother. That mother's name was Taylor.

When a publicity party was given for Roddy McDowall, and Elizabeth Taylor was invited, her mother tried to get a date for her from among Howard's friends, and rare is the teenage boy who will gladly date a girl at her mother's request.

The Taylors threw a party for every teenager they could find—a backyard barbecue—and got irritated when their guests, toward sundown, started necking. (Elizabeth Taylor wasn't among the neckers, not with her mother quite so noticeably present.) Mrs. Taylor wandered around the backyard, ringing a bell and ousting the neckers. And she couldn't figure out why her intensive efforts and ubiquitous presence weren't resulting in dates for her daughter. But the worst was yet to some. The Taylors rented a house at Malibu Beach for the summer, and Elizabeth Taylor went to her first grunion run.

To a non-Californian, the grunion sounds like a fictitious beast, similar to the goonie bird or the sea serpent, but grunion really do exist, and the grunion run is a well-established California custom.

The grunion is a fish, somewhat similar to a smelt, but with spawning habits more like that of salmon. At certain times, the female grunion gather in thousands and thousands at the crest of a wave coming in toward the beach. When the wave breaks on the beach, the grunion stay behind to lay their eggs in the wet sand. The *next* wave brings in the male grunion, and sweeps the female grunion back out to sea. The male grunion fertilize the eggs left behind by the females, and are themselves washed back out to sea in their turn.

The grunion run is a fantastic sight, and the temptation to dash down to the edge of the sea and try to catch one or two of them between waves is irresistible. Gradually, over the years, the grunion run has become a social occasion. The local newspapers report when a grunion run is due—it is possible for the weather bureau to predict a grunion run in advance, with a number of variable factors to be considered—and local citizens and tourists alike congregate on the beach, around bonfires, ostensibly to catch the grunion but actually to neck. Grunion-hunters come in pairs, one male and one female.

Elizabeth Taylor may have been the only teenage girl in history to be accompanied on a grunion run by her mother and father.

8

SHORTLY BEFORE HER SIXTEENTH BIRTHDAY, life began to change once more for Elizabeth Taylor. To begin with, she finally got herself a date.

There were a few certain things that could have been predicted about Elizabeth Taylor's first date. That the boy would be someone connected with the studio. That the date itself would be well publicized. And that Mother would be along.

The predictions, had they been made, would have come true. The boy who was Elizabeth Taylor's first date escort was Marshall Thompson, himself a teenage actor contracted to MGM. He didn't ask Elizabeth Taylor personally, but approached her mother instead, apparently realizing that the important answer to his question would come from her.

The question: He had two tickets to the premiere of *The Yearling*, Did Mrs. Taylor mind if he asked Elizabeth to go with him?

Mrs. Taylor didn't mind at all. In fact, it just so happened that she had a pair of tickets to the same premiere. She would take Marshall Thompson's mother as *her* guest, and they could make it a foursome!

That was the first of a series of dates between Elizabeth Taylor and Marshall Thompson. After the first date, they were left on their own for most of the rest of them, and it became apparent that a ridiculous, frustrating and humiliating phase—Elizabeth Taylor unable to get any dates—had finally come to an end.

At just around the same time, another phase in Elizabeth Taylor's life was drawing to a close: She was no longer a twixt-and-between. She was old enough to get back into an active role in movie-making.

MGM, at this time—1948 and 1949—considered Elizabeth Taylor a million-dollar investment which was now about to start paying off. Just as they had moved with extreme care when this investment had entered the dangerous years, they now moved with similar great care in bringing her out of the dangerous years again.

Her return to active movie-making was fanfared with as much publicity as the studio drum beaters could stir up. Articles appeared in national magazines around the theme, "Elizabeth Taylor Grows Up—Becomes A Mature And Beautiful Woman." Her first movie, *Cynthia,* was sloganed, *"Her First Kiss!"* (A few years later, Elizabeth Taylor told a reporter her first kiss had actually arrived via Marshall Thompson a few days before the celluloid kiss was filmed.)

In the space of one year after returning to films, Elizabeth Taylor was cast in five motion pictures, and her roles in these five films made a careful, slow progression in age. She played a girl of sixteen in *Cynthia*, followed by the seventeen-year-old visiting cousin in *Life with Father*, then an eighteen-year-old in *A Date with Judy*. This was followed by a role as Greer Garson's twenty-year-old daughter in *Julia Misbehaves*, and culminated in her first serious adult role as Robert Taylor's wife in *Conspirator*, shot on location in England.

After the first movie kiss in *Cynthia*, the second had to wait until *Julie Misbehaves*, which she played opposite Peter Lawford. "I had a slight crush on him," she said later, speaking of Lawford, "and I became so flustered when he kissed me that I got bright red, while the crew went into hysterics."

Between the filming of *Life with Father* and *A Date with Judy*, the publicity department moved into high gear. This was Elizabeth Taylor's comeback—as an *adult* star—and the studio was determined not to trip up as it had done so often in the past with grown-up child stars. Elizabeth Taylor and her mother went on a well-publicized jaunt to England, surrounded by banks of photographers. On their return, in September of 1947, they went to Cambridge, Massachusetts, to Harvard University, for a banquet in honor of the Harvard *Advocate*, the university's oldest student publication. The *Advocate's* editorial staff had chosen Elizabeth Taylor the "actress most likely to succeed," their "favorite lady," made her an honorary editor of the paper, and awarded her the Harvard *Advocate* medal.

Just as accidents had marred her first brief period of movie-making and the transitional years, so sickness accompanied her at the beginning of her career as an adult star. On the *Queen Mary*, sailing to England during the publicity trip of the summer of 1947, a number of passengers—

Elizabeth Taylor inevitably among them—came down with severe stomach cramps and high fever. She had a temperature of one hundred and four during the entire sea voyage, and then spent the first week of this three-week trip to England bedridden.

After the trip to England, and the quadruple presentation from the Harvard *Advocate,* Elizabeth Taylor returned to Toyland to make *A Date with Judy* with Jane Powell and *Julia Misbehaves* with Greer Garson, Walter Pidgeon and Peter Lawford, which completed the first phase of the studio's plan for her comeback in motion pictures. In *Cynthia,* she had been reintroduced to the vast movie-going public, and her comeback was virtually all set. This was followed by *Life with Father* and *A Date with Judy,* in both of which she played good-sized supporting roles, for in these films rapid repeat exposure to the audience was the main objective. Then, with three movies already in circulation, with the fact that she had grown up carefully established, she played opposite Peter Lawford in *Julia Misbehaves,* in which, as a twenty-year-old girl, she was kissed by Lawford and, in the script, eloped with him.

Her sixteenth birthday occurred during the filming of *Julia Misbehaves.* The Ford convertible she had been given two years before—but which she had never been allowed to drive—had apparently wasted away from disuse. For her sixteenth birthday, she was given a blue Cadillac with keys made of solid gold. Consistent with the inconsistent quality of her life, she wasn't allowed to drive this car either, not for almost a year, till she was nearly seventeen years of age. When permission to drive the Cadillac was granted, it had a rider: so must she. She couldn't drive the car alone.

Only one thing was lacking for the publicity campaign to be complete: a real-life boyfriend. Though dates were not as infrequent any more as they had once been—Marshall Thompson, Jerome Courtland, Roddy McDowall and Tommy Breene were among her escorts at this time—there wasn't any one particular romantic interest in her life. The studio publicity department and Mrs. Taylor, working together, cleared potential escorts for appearance, background, character and newsworthiness, introduced the ones who were passed on to Elizabeth Taylor, and sat back waiting for sparks to fly. Mrs. Taylor made press announcements of all of her daughter's dates, and the studio publicity department kept waiting impatiently for Cupid to strike.

For a long while, nothing happened. She went out on occasional dates, well chaperoned by press agents and photographers and other flacks, and Cupid (perhaps intimidated by the flashbulbs) kept his distance. But then Glenn Davis, Army's famous football star, happened.

It was inevitable that Elizabeth Taylor and Glenn Davis should be introduced to one another by someone from the studio publicity department. The individual was Doris Kearns. She and her husband brought Davis to the Taylors' summer home at Malibu Beach. This time, the sparks flew, and *everybody* was happy.

Elizabeth Taylor and Glenn Davis had seven dates together. This was the extent of their "romance," but it was about as well publicized as World War II.

One of their dates was to the *Times* benefit football game. During this "date," Glenn Davis was seated on one side of her and Doris Kearns, her publicist, sat with her husband on the other side. The date had been so well publicized that the entire stadium of spectators knew the couple was there—unfortunately for the publicity department, it was a football game and not a movie premiere, so the crowd limited itself to shouts of, "We want Davis!" The other six dates between Elizabeth Taylor and Glenn Davis were all at just about the same level of quiet privacy.

After the seventh date, Davis, then a lieutenant in the Army, was shipped to Korea. He had been on his pre-overseas leave when they'd met. He gave her, as a keepsake, his small gold All-America football on a chain, for her to wear around her neck.

In the inevitable press interview, the sixteen-year-old Elizabeth Taylor said, "We've engaged to be engaged." She showed photographs of the engagement ring Davis had bought her. She couldn't show the ring itself; her mother thought she was too young to wear it.

9

SIXTEEN IS A FRAIL AND FICKLE AGE. Forced lengthy separation of lovers can easily be disastrous to their love, particularly when before that separation they had seen one another less than a dozen times and only when chaperoned by half the photographers and flacks of Toyland.

Glenn Davis went to Korea. (This was 1948, two years before the Korean police action, so that separation of the lovers wasn't balanced by any particular danger to either of them.) Elizabeth Taylor went to England to star in her first serious adult role opposite Robert Taylor in *Conspirator.*

It was during this five-month stay in England that she first met Michael Wilding whom, four years later, she was to marry. At this time, however, she was still wearing Glenn Davis' gold football, and she was still writing him frequent letters.

At thirty-six—twenty years her senior—Wilding was a handsome and famous British actor, who would a year later win a poll as England's most popular male actor. Though she spent her evenings writing letters to Glenn Davis, her days were partially given over to flirting with Wilding. Wilding later described this studio lunchroom flirtation in this manner: "Rather than ask the waitress for some salt, she'd walk clear through the commissary to get it from the kitchen, wiggling her hips. Then she'd wiggle her way back."

"That was for your benefit alone, darling," she told him during their marriage, "even if it didn't work."

Though Wilding had been recently separated from his wife, he was still technically married. And the age difference at that time was far greater than it would be in four years. As a result, when Elizabeth Taylor returned to the United States there was no hint of any Taylor-Wilding romance.

Back in America, Elizabeth Taylor celebrated her seventeenth birthday with her mother at the Florida home of her wealthy art dealer great-uncle, Howard Young, who had once, years before, employed her father as his European representative. During her stay in Florida, she met William D. Pawley, Jr., twenty-eight years of age, vice-president of his father's bus company. The Pawleys were wealthy and socially prominent, and Pawley, Sr. had once been ambassador to Brazil.

William D. Pawley, Jr. passed Mrs. Taylor's screening process, met Mrs. Taylor's daughter, and the gold football went back to Glenn Davis. But this, too, was grist for the publicity mill, and the fact that Glenn and Liz weren't going to be married, after all, was headlined across the country.

Shortly thereafter, another wave of headlines announced the fact that she had become engaged to Bill Pawley. This time, Mrs. Taylor considered her daughter old enough to wear the ring—3½ carats—which saved carting a lot of bulky photographs around from interview to interview.

At seventeen, Elizabeth Taylor was working on her second engagement. She had made ten motion pictures. She was a million-dollar property. She was also completely a product of Toyland, a strange amalgam of child and woman. In some ways, she was ten years of age; in other ways, she was thirty; in no way at all was she seventeen.

One incident which took place at the end of the *Conspirator* filming in England illustrates this child-woman quality rather well. Shooting of the picture had finished a week early, leaving the Taylors plenty of time before they were to sail back to the States aboard the *Queen Elizabeth.* They wanted to spend part of that time shopping in Paris, but there was a flu epidemic in France at the time and the studio, well aware of Elizabeth Taylor's proneness to accident and disease, refused its paternal permission. Elizabeth Taylor wrote the following petition, which she then wheedled most of the employees at the London studio to sign:

> We, the undersigned, agree with Elizabeth Taylor that she *should* be allowed to go to Paris on a shopping spree . . .
>
> Inasmuch as she has promised
>
> 1. To be a good girl,
> 2. To shun all flu germs,
> 3. Not to contract even as much as a runny nose . . .
>
> Her sole purpose in going to Paris is to acquire a few handmade pink unmentionables, gloves, handkerchiefs, etc.
>
> We feel that this *Most Necessary* Trip should *not be denied* her.

She herself added half a dozen gag signatures ("Lord Byron, Scarlett O'Hara") to this petition and then, with Michael Wilding's help, got the rest of the real-life signatures, including one from Mrs. Ben Goetz, wife of the head of the London studio, the man who had said no in the first place.

She got to Paris. Cuteness *always* works in Toyland. Even when you're all grown up.

The engagement to Bill Pawley didn't last long. It was only after it had been announced to the press, and had received the normal clatter of headlines that was beginning to accompany every event in Elizabeth Taylor's young life, that Pawley revealed the reason for the breakup.

He wanted his wife-to-be to quit her job.

Bill Pawley could afford to keep a wife in just about any style, accustomed or not. And he had the old-fashioned notion that it was the husband's job to bring home the bacon, that a man married a woman and not a million-dollar property.

Apparently, Elizabeth Taylor found a certain fascination in these revolutionary ideas, at least at first. But the combined influence of her mother and the studio was too strong. Shortly after the announcement of the engagement, Mrs. Taylor hurried her daughter back to Toyland. MGM cast her immediately in *The Big Hangover,* opposite Van Johnson, to try to take her mind off Pawley and his medieval notions.

The attempt worked, but it took a while. During the shooting of *The Big Hangover,* she spent hours nearly every night on long-distance phone calls to Bill in Florida. The phone calls continued when, with the completion of that picture, she was sent on loan-out to Paramount for *A Place in the Sun.* However, *A Place in the Sun* was the second picture in Elizabeth Taylor's career which she enjoyed making. With the studio protecting its million-dollar property with militant care, and with Elizabeth Taylor herself at last involved in a motion picture she could enjoy and respect, the case of Bill Pawley, three thousand miles away, was doomed.

Realizing this, Pawley hurried to California, but it was too late. His fiancée was still a little girl in many respects; every decision of her life thus far had been made for her by her mother or the studio. Through the Coventry punishment that had pervaded her childhood, she had grown up terrified of rejection, afraid to assert herself for fear the result would be a denial of her as an individual, an actual person. She combined this fear with an as-yet-unspoiled trust in her mother's judgment and the judgment of the studio executives.

According to Mrs. Taylor: "I think Elizabeth realized for the first time how much she really loved being in pictures. Not just for the glamour, or the money, or the fun of it, but because it kept her in touch with the world and people."

The world. Toyland.

10

THIS WAS ELIZABETH TAYLOR'S second broken engagement in less than a year. Though she was still being built up via an unrelenting publicity campaign as the new *grown-up* Elizabeth Taylor, there was nevertheless the strong implication in all the publicity that she was as sweet and unpretentious as ever. (A feature article in the New York *Times* for January 2, 1949 had called her, ". . . a soft-spoken, quiet, rather shy young girl who hasn't sought any of the artistic and financial rewards she has reaped. They have simply come her way.")

As a result, Bill Pawley was asked to make the announcement of the broken engagement, to take at least a part of the onus from Elizabeth Taylor. He did so, first staying in California long enough to go with her to Jane Powell's wedding. He left after the wedding, and made the announcement after he'd returned to Florida.

However, things didn't work out quite as well this time as Mrs. Taylor or the studio publicity department hoped.

The press by now believed that Elizabeth Taylor *was* grown up, and so the journalists' attitude toward her underwent a subtle change. There is one inflexible rule when reporting the doings of a child star: If you have nothing good to say, don't say anything at all. The same rule does not apply to *grown-up* stars. Another rule comes into play: Anything that moves is news; anything that slinks is hot news.

The Taylor family wasn't used to that sort of thing, and didn't plan their actions accordingly. They assumed that they had covered themselves as much as necessary when they'd asked Bill Pawley to make the announcement that the engagement had ended. After that, they lived their own lives, without the jungle wariness that must eventually become second nature to every adult celebrity.

Bill Pawley and the Taylor family went to Jane Powell's wedding, and then Pawley left, for the airport and home. Mr. and Mrs. Taylor took Elizabeth, who had reacted to the parting emotionally, with the bridesmaids and ushers of the wedding to a night club, the Mocambo, where Vic Damone was singing. They had met Damone earlier that day, at the wedding.

Sitting at the table in the Mocambo, Elizabeth Taylor burst into tears. Damone sang one song particularly for her, in an effort to cheer her up, and then sat at the table with her after his show was finished.

The following morning, in Florida, Bill Pawley announced to the press that his engagement to Elizabeth Taylor was called off. The ladies and gentlemen of the press looked around to see how Miss Taylor was taking it all, and discovered that she had been seen just the night before in the Mocambo—with Vic Damone. The newspaper stories about the broken engagement were somewhat snide: "Off with the old love and on with the new."

Elizabeth Taylor was having her first taste of bad press. It wasn't to be the last.

The repercussions of the evening spent at the Mocambo were not yet done. Conrad Nicholson Hilton, Jr., son of the multimillionaire hotel owner, had also been there that night. He had seen Elizabeth Taylor there and had determined to meet her. He knew Peter Freeman, whose father was a top executive at Paramount where Elizabeth Taylor was working in *A Place in the Sun,* and through this contact he wangled an introduction. After he had been successfully screened by Mrs. Taylor, he came to the set with Peter Freeman and his wife, was introduced to Elizabeth Taylor, and the four of them went to lunch together. On their return, Mrs. Taylor asked her daughter, "Did you have a nice time, honey?"

Her reply was listless: "I guess so."

When Nick Hilton phoned the next day, asking for a date, she asked him to the Taylor home for dinner. Mrs. Taylor explains, "She never accepted invitations or made dates until the young men had been at our house and met with our approval. We had made this a rule when she was much younger and she continued it."

The son of Conrad Hilton was, of course, eminently approvable. He was also smitten with Elizabeth Taylor. He gave up smoking and drinking and stopped running around.

Since Elizabeth Taylor was still carrying something of a torch for Bill Pawley, Nick Hilton's dates with her were at first confined to dinner meetings, sometimes with her parents and sometimes with his, and often all four parents were present.

At around the same time, another well-known playboy became aware of the fact that Elizabeth Taylor really *had* grown up, and went about arranging an introduction to her. This one was Howard Hughes, the multimillionaire moviemaker and airplane manufacturer. Seeing Elizabeth Taylor walking through the lobby of the Beverly Hills Hotel, be turned to his assistant, Johnny Meyer, and said, "Get me an introduction to that girl."

During the 1947 Senate investigation of Howard Hughes and his aircraft companies, Meyer had become well known as a man who knew an incredible number of girls in Hollywood, but Elizabeth Taylor was not on his list. Nevertheless, he followed her and saw her enter her father's art gallery which was situated in the Beverly Hills Hotel. Meyer arranged with an employee of the hotel to meet Francis Taylor—and, incidentally, his daughter—and then it was only one more step for Meyer to bring Hughes into the art gallery and make the required introductions.

Hughes bought two paintings from Francis Taylor, and then invited Mr. and Mrs. Taylor—and their daughter—to dinner with him. The invitation was accepted, and was the first of many dinners involving Hughes and Elizabeth Taylor, chaperoned by her parents.

At just about the same time, therefore, Elizabeth Taylor was being courted in exactly the same courtly manner—dinner invitations with the folks—by two totally different men, twenty-two-year-old Nick Hilton and forty-four-year-old Howard Hughes. The gossip columns were full of the Taylor-Hilton romance. Not one word was printed of the

Taylor-Hughes courting—though every columnist was aware of it and so was every nervous MGM executive—until nearly seven years after the fact.

Mr. and Mrs. Taylor have never expressed their opinions publicly concerning the courting of their daughter by Howard Hughes. Elizabeth Taylor made *her* opinion crystal clear at the time the courtship was going on. Hughes bored her, and she didn't try to hide the fact. It may have been this indifference that, at least partially, attracted Hughes, who was used to being able to choose his women from an inexhaustible supply.

Aside from the dinners he hosted for the Taylor family, Hughes also spent a weekend with the Taylors in Reno. In addition, he badgered all of their mutual friends to give dinner parties to which both of them could be invited.

This schoolboyishness was self-defeating. When asked to a dinner party, Elizabeth Taylor took to replying, "If Howard is coming, I'm not."

Nick Hilton, on the other hand, was doing much better. From an initial indifference to him that rivaled her indifference to Hughes, Elizabeth Taylor gradually came to like Hilton and later to love him.

The similarities between Nick Hilton and Bill Pawley were, of course, many, down to the "Jr." at the end of both their names. Both were handsome, in their twenties, the sons of wealthy men. Both had traveled extensively—Nick had worked in various of his father's hotels from the age of fourteen, had served a hitch in the Navy as an enlisted man, and then spent time studying at a hotel school in Switzerland—and both were entertaining raconteurs of their travels. Both were working in their father's businesses—Nick was at the time vice-president and manager of the Bel-Air Hotel—but neither allowed business to interfere with pleasure.

There was only one significant difference between Nick Hilton and Bill Pawley: Nick Hilton did not insist that his wife give up her career to marry him.

Countering Howard Hughes' Reno weekend, Hilton invited the Taylors to Texas, to the Hilton hotel at Arrowhead Springs, for New Year's. After a week at Hilton Sr.'s Arrowhead Lake home, the Taylors returned to Hollywood, where it became plain that Elizabeth Taylor's indifference had come to an end.

And so matters stood when Elizabeth Taylor's eighteenth birthday arrived, on February 27th of 1950. This birthday was like all the others in Toyland, in that it was extravagantly noticed and recorded, but in the real world outside it was significantly different from every birthday before it. Eighteen is the youngest self-determination age in California. By California law, Elizabeth Taylor was no longer a minor.

She could collect her own salary. Until then, according to law, her parents had collected and invested her salary, in cooperation with a judge, and not one penny of it had been spent for anything. At the age of seventeen, she had still been living on an allowance of fifty cents a week, though, of course, she was given clothing and automobiles, and most of her dining out was at the publicity department's expense. Between the fifty cents a week in cash and the almost unlimited funds in credit at her disposal, she came to her legal maturity with virtually no knowledge or ability in the handling of money, a fact that would plague her in years to come.

In addition to financial independence, Elizabeth Taylor's eighteenth birthday gave her full legal independence in every other way as well. She was no longer legally *required* to obey her mother's will.

Therefore, when Elizabeth Taylor married Nick Hilton sixty-eight days after her eighteenth birthday, May 6, 1950, it was generally accepted in the movie colony that she was revolting against her mother, but this seems unlikely. Immediately after her birthday, when she had first started receiving her own salary of $2,000 a week, she had hurried out and bought her mother a Cadillac, her father a Chevrolet, and had paid half the cost of a Ford for her brother. When she was asked years later, if she had married Hilton as a form of revolt from her mother, she replied, "No, that isn't true, or I'd have married one of my other fiancés. I was terribly in love with Nicky, in a completely idealistic way."

At the time, she had been voluble on the subject. "This time I'm *really* in love," she told the reporters. Asked what she and Nick Hilton had in common as a basis for marriage, she answered, "We both love hamburgers with onions, oversized sweaters and Pinza."

The wedding was arranged by MGM, with all the loving care (and love of spectacle) more normally lavished on an MGM musical. It was gala, gorgeous, gigantic and grotesque. Helen Rose, an MGM costume designer, created the wedding gown—satin embroidered with pearls. A fleet of MGM limousines carried the wedding party to the church, where MGM policemen held back the crowd of 2,500 fans alerted to the wedding by an "accidental leak" months before. Inside the church, there was a star-studded cast; Fred Astaire, Ginger Rogers, Esther Williams, Greer Garson, Dick Powell,

June Allyson, Phil Harris, Alice Faye, Ann Miller and Janet Leigh were among the seven hundred celebrities crammed into the church.

The church was the Roman Catholic Church of the Good Shepherd in Beverly Hills, and Monsignor Patrick J. Concannon officiated. Nick Hilton was a Roman Catholic, Elizabeth Taylor was from a Christian Science family.

After the ceremony, the couple spent a week at Carmel-by-the-Sea, returned—incredibly enough—to spend Mother's Day with their two mothers, and then went on to what the press described as a "dream honeymoon" in Europe, lasting five months.

The marriage lasted two months longer than that.

11

On December 14, 1950, the legal department at MGM made an announcement over Elizabeth Taylor's name. It read, in part, "I am very sorry that Nick and I are unable to adjust our differences, and that we have come to a final parting of the ways. We both regret this decision, but after personal discussions we realize there is no possibility of a reconciliation."

Seven months and eight days after MGM had starred her in a marriage, Elizabeth Taylor was about to sue for a divorce. And the "father" studio was there as always, ready, willing and able, prepared to handle the divorce with the same professional flair that had been displayed in the handling of the marriage.

Unfortunately, the cast didn't go through its paces in as orderly a manner this time around and, gradually, bits of truth began to protrude through the technicolor curtain 'round Toyland. The girl got emotional—she was only shedding a husband, but she refused to see it in a proper Toyland perspective—and the divorce got messy.

The honeymoon, it seemed, hadn't *really* lasted five months. Technically, since this was the length of time the couple spent in Europe, it was also the length of the honeymoon. Actually, the honeymoon was over much sooner than that.

Shortly after Mr. and Mrs. Hilton had arrived in Europe, signs of a rift began to appear. Hotel employees told reporters about bitter quarrels in the honeymoon suite. Nick spent far too much time at the gambling tables, while his new wife waited for him, either in a corner of the casino or in the suite. Nick had started drinking again. Mrs. Hilton, who had never smoked before, became a chain-smoker. She lost twenty pounds during the "honeymoon," and came back to Hollywood sadder and wiser, but determined still to make a marriage of what was essentially an adolescent adventure.

Later, she was to say of this first marriage, "When I married Nick, I fell off my pink cloud with a thud."

People were supposed to live *happily* ever after in Toyland.

Returning to California, they settled in a rented house, and both went back to their prior modes of life as much as possible. Hilton devoted his attention to the hotel of which he was manager and to golf. Elizabeth Taylor reported to the studio and went to work on *Father's Little Dividend.* But the quarrels continued, and finally she walked out.

"We were both much too young and immature," she said some years later, "and our European honeymoon lasted five months, which is too long. We had no feeling of security or settling down. Until I was married, I had never before spent a night away from my mother."

When at last she left Hilton, she was on the verge of a nervous breakdown. After eighteen years of having all of life softened for her by people who considered her too valuable *to them* to be exposed to the harshness of reality, she wasn't at all prepared for life with an easily bored adolescent.

However, the damage had been done. She tried to go home and couldn't. The diet of emotional saccharine fed her by her mother—plus Mrs. Taylor's insistence that her daughter's marriage *not* end in a divorce which could do irreparable damage to her career—was too much for a girl who had now been exposed to the harsh glare of the world outside Toyland. She left her mother's home, too.

For the next few weeks, she was a nervous, pathetic wanderer, staying at the house of one friend after another. There were times when a friend of hers would receive a tearful, distraught phone call from her at midnight, begging to be allowed to camp for the night on a living room sofa. Among the people who took her in were her stand-in, Margery Dillon; the MGM costume designer who had made her wedding dress, Helen Rose; and her agent, Jules Goldstone, and his wife.

At the same time, she was finishing *Father's Little Dividend.* The studio had used work as a therapy with her before and it had succeeded, so they tried the treatment again, putting her to work, immediately after the completion of *Father's Little Dividend,* on another film, ironically titled *Love Is Better Than Ever.* This time, however, instead of easing the situation, it only served to complicate it further, for it introduced her to the director of the film, Stanley Donen, twenty-seven years old, himself recently divorced. Donen was an intelligent and sympathetic listener, and was soon a compelling influence, threatening the power of both Mrs. Taylor and the studio.

Mrs. Taylor was nearly as distraught as her daughter. Divorce was unthinkable. Stanley Donen was equally unthinkable. And Elizabeth wouldn't even come home, where she belonged!

Mrs. Taylor had her own explanation for her daughter's having gone to such desperate lengths to find some place to sleep other than her parents' home: "She went to her stand-in, Margery Dillon, instead of coming home, so that no one could say that she had 'run home to mother.'"

As for Nick Hilton, once Elizabeth Taylor left him he decided he wanted her, after all. He hunted her down at whatever friend's house she was currently staying, then sent roses by the bushelful and kept phoning until she tottered out into the night again, looking for some other refuge.

On the set of *Love Is Better Than Ever,* she appeared white-faced and painfully thin, trembling with fatigue and nerves. Often she would burst suddenly into tears; whenever that happened, Donen would dismiss the cast for the day and offer his sympathetic ear to be talked at and a shoulder to cry on.

Finally, in the early part of December, she made the decision to divorce Hilton. She was staying with Mr. and Mrs. Goldstone at the time and, with their approval, called Hilton and asked him to come see her, since she felt it necessary to tell him face to face of her decision to sue for divorce.

He came at once, and the two of them spent more than an hour closeted together in the den. Then Goldstone heard young Nick Hilton shouting, ranting and raving at his wife, and when this continued with no end in sight Goldstone stepped in and suggested that Nick leave. Then the studio was informed of Elizabeth Taylor's decision, and the studio legal department drafted the announcement, which was made public on December 15th. Nine days later, the divorce suit was begun. Her plea was mental cruelty, and she asked for no alimony.

If the Taylor-Hilton wedding was handled by MGM in the style of a musical extravaganza, the Taylor-Hilton divorce was handled—by MGM—with the underplayed suavity of a British-style courtroom drama. Nothing could be heard but the quiet meshing of gears and muted clicks as relays fell softly into place.

Until the plaintiff took the stand.

She started well enough. Her lawyer calmly questioned her, and quietly she answered his questions, and gradually the story of the eight-month-old marriage emerged. Nick Hilton had ignored her almost from the beginning, had started drinking heavily shortly after their arrival in Europe, had spent most of his time gambling and had had as little as possible to do with her.

The story was emerging gradually enough and quietly enough, but only for a while. Then the reality of the memory of what she was describing began to get to Elizabeth Taylor, whose nerves were already in terrible shape from her past few nomadic months and her involvement with *Love Is Better Than Ever*, a poor pot-boiler of a movie which she hated intensely.

At last she cried, "I've the body of a woman and the emotions of a child!" and burst into tears. She couldn't continue her testimony, and was sobbing so violently she had to be excused from the stand while her lawyer finished telling the story himself.

On January 29, 1951, the divorce was granted. The marriage that had started sixty-eight days after Elizabeth Taylor's eighteenth birthday ended twenty-nine days before her nineteenth birthday, a total of eight months and twenty-three days in all.

Elizabeth Taylor was not yet a revolutionary, but she had just engaged in an involuntary revolution, partly the result of her marriage, partly the result of her changed legal situation now that she had come of age. Virtually her entire life had suddenly been rearranged. From a personal cash spendable income of fifty cents a week, she now had a spendable income of two thousand dollars a week. From a virginal ingenue tied by apron strings of invisible iron to her mother, she was now a divorcee who found it impossible, for the sake of her nerves, to live at home with her mother. From a child star whose foibles—if any—would be treated indulgently by the studio and circumspectly by the press, she had become an adult star expected to work on *Love Is Better Than Ever* whether she liked it or not, and able to pick up a newspaper or a movie magazine and read, from time to time, rather harsh criticism of her actions.

Toyland was hardly the same place any more.

BOOK III

Elizabeth and Michael

12

THOUGH TOYLAND had undergone some revolutionary changes, it was nevertheless still Toyland, and Elizabeth Taylor was still very much a part of it. And, though she was no longer living at home, she was still very much under the influence of her mother.

This influence was nearly shattered over the problem of Stanley Donen. Mrs. Taylor and the studio executives were in unanimous agreement on this subject: Stanley Donen was a fine person, but he was not going to be Elizabeth Taylor's second husband, and that was all there was to it. Mrs. Taylor made this clear to her daughter, and was startled to find that she was meeting with strong and high-strung resistance. Elizabeth Taylor had become more dependent on Donen than anyone had realized.

At the same tune, her nervous condition had eventually resulted in physical illness, a severe case of colitis. "I was ordered by doctors to eat nothing but strained baby food, and I grew thinner and thinner," she said later of this period.

Donen, whom she was seeing every day on the set of *Love Is Better Than Ever,* treated her with careful sympathy while at the same time managing to get *some* work done on the film every day. After Mrs. Taylor's near-disastrous attempt to intervene in this deepening relationship, the studio maintained a circumspect hands-off policy. The girl was too upset to be argued with now—she might fight back and discover that she could win—and besides, Donen was managing to keep her working. There was, the studio hoped with fingers crossed, plenty of time to spare. Once *Love Is Better Than Ever* was in the can, something could be done about the Donen situation.

One of the studio executives summed it up this way: "A number of us thought that Donen was a fine guy, but not for Elizabeth."

In the meantime, Elizabeth Taylor was suddenly homeless, for the first time in her life. She found it impossible to return to her parents' home—her nerves were in bad enough shape as it was—but at the same time she couldn't stand to live alone. Her agent, Jules Goldstone, suggested she hire a secretary-companion, and further recommended a friend of his own secretary's, a woman named Peggy Rutledge who had once worked as secretary to Mrs. Bob Hope. Elizabeth Taylor agreed and Goldstone arranged for them to meet in his office.

Peggy Rutledge later described the meeting thus: "I asked Elizabeth what we should talk about. She said she hadn't the slightest idea. Then, she suddenly asked if I could make coffee; it turned out neither of us could cook. Finally I said, 'Well, let's try sharing an apartment. If you don't like me, I'll leave. If I don't like you, I'll also leave.'"

They found a five-room furnished apartment on Wilshire Boulevard and moved into it in March of 1951, a month and a half after the Hilton divorce. Then, with cheerful and matter-of-fact Peggy Rutledge at home and compassionate Stanley Donen at the studio, it was possible for Elizabeth Taylor to try to get herself on an even keel again. The colitis, however, continued as severe as ever.

Love Is Better Than Ever was finally finished, and just barely in time, for Elizabeth Taylor and Stanley Donen were beginning to admit openly to one another that they were in love.

Said a studio executive: "We agreed that the best way to separate them was to send her abroad to make a picture. She got the role of Rebecca in *Ivanhoe* and she left for London that June."

With her went Peggy Rutledge and a full supply of strained baby food. She had no idea the studio was simply getting her away from Donen, and the two of them went dancing together a few times before she had to leave Hollywood.

She arrived in London a frail and frazzled wreck, unhappy, unsure of herself, absolutely lost in a world turned upside down. Richard Thorpe, who directed *Ivanhoe,* met her on arrival and said, "Then and later, I expected her to break down any minute."

She didn't break down. Just as Stanley Donen had come into the picture to lend her his own strength after she had given up her husband and found it impossible to return to her mother, so another man stepped forward in London to offer her his direction, guidance and strength—Michael Wilding. "I thought I'd influence this trembling little creature," he said later. "I thought I'd guide her along life's stony path."

Wilding called her the day she arrived in London, explaining, "I honestly thought she might be lonely." She accepted and, according to Wilding, "With Peggy Rutledge, we went to dinner that night and for the next five."

To which Elizabeth Taylor added, "And without Peggy Rutledge from then on."

This was not the first meeting between the two since her sixteen-year-old flirtation with him nearly four years earlier. He had been in Hollywood just a few months before, making his first American movie. They had met then but, as Wilding said, "Stanley Donen was then the love of her life. I used to see them dancing in night clubs."

In London, there was no Stanley Donen in the way. Wilding called, she accepted, and a romance was born. "At the sight of him," she said later, "I decided to forget my baby food. I ate anything I liked, and in a month I was cured of all my ailments."

This is one of the illnesses her critics point to as being fraudulent, because of the readiness with which it disappeared when she became interested in Michael Wilding. There seems little doubt that this colitis and a number of later afflictions that hit her at strategic times were of psychosomatic origin—that is, the physical side-effects of nervous frustration—but there is a great difference between *psychosomatic* and *fraudulent* illnesses. In the latter, the individual is consciously inventing a nonexistent suffering. In the former, mental or nervous suffering is transformed, without conscious volition of the victim, into actual physical suffering.

For instance, in the winter of 1960 Elizabeth Taylor was suddenly admitted to a London hospital, screaming with pain and suffering from a high fever. A reporter quoted her as saying, "Maybe now people will believe I am *really* sick—and not blame everything on me." In the hospital it was at first thought that she was suffering from spinal meningitis, but after a spinal tap it was discovered that what she had was actually meningism—the *symptoms* of meningitis, in other words, without the actual sickness.

Meningism is not fraudulent. Nor is it completely physical. It can be an unconscious plea for sympathy and understanding, the result of mental or nervous tension.

The thing is, Elizabeth Taylor grew up in a world in which she was pampered and protected, a valuable piece of property whose every ailment was of immediate and intense concern. In addition, sickness of one form or another was the only way—aside from a written note of apology or acquiescence—that she as a child could get out of Coventry and be noticed again by her mother and her governess. It would have been impossible for her to grow up without the subconscious realization that ill health was just about the best weapon she had for getting her own way.

During the Hilton divorce, and until her trip to England, her colitis served an important function, that of gaining and keeping sympathy for herself. She was, after all, the plaintiff in the divorce case. *She* was the one who had given up trying to make a success of her marriage in less than eight months. *She* was the one about whom most of the publicity would center. *She* was the one whose career might be destroyed.

At the same time, recurring physical pain made it possible to end conversations with her mother abruptly without being rude. Her illness made it possible to quit work on *Love Is better Than Ever*—a picture she loathed—whenever it became too irritating. And, of course, the colitis was an additional hold on Stanley Donen's sympathy.

This doesn't mean to imply that the colitis was faked. It was not. It was an actual physical disease, but its *causes* were not physical, they were neural and emotional.

When the neural and emotional causative agents were relieved, the colitis inevitably faded away. Once Elizabeth Taylor was in England, with an important role in an important motion picture, it had become clear that the divorce had *not* ruined her career, that the publicity surrounding the divorce had been, for the most part, favorable, and that she was not now going to be relegated to roles in films like *Love Is Better Than Ever.* Also, her mother was not with her—this was her second trip without her mother, the first being the ill-fated honeymoon with Nick Hilton—so sickness was no longer needed as a tactful way to end the flow of advice. And Stanley Donen, of course, was six thousand miles away, while Michael Wilding was very present.

This last may have been the most important factor of all. Wilding liked a good time—good food and good company, posh clothes and posh surroundings, sparkling conversations and lots of laughter—and wasn't long on the sickbed routine. A moaning little girl with colitis was best left to her own devices; Michael Wilding could always find more entertaining company than *that.*

The colitis disappeared.

Elizabeth Taylor and Michael Wilding dated frequently during the filming of *Ivanhoe,* and soon decided they were in love. Two years earlier, after breaking the engagement with

Bill Pawley, she had said, "I guess I'm just in love with love." Now she seemed intent on proving that earlier statement. Six months after breaking up with one vivacious playboy, she proposed marriage to another one, twice the age of the first.

"I finally proposed to him," she stated in an interview five years later. "He was everything I admired in a man, and I thought him remarkable. We'd already said we loved each other, earlier. But he said I was too young, I'd change my mind. When I objected, he said we should wait."

They waited another six months, but not as a result of a caution that would have been uncharacteristic in either of them. There were sound legal reasons for waiting. In the first place, it takes a year to get a final decree in a California divorce, and the year was not yet up. In the second place, Wilding already had a wife, from whom he'd been separated for four years, and he'd have to see about divorcing that one before gaining another.

In the fall, the location work for *Ivanhoe* was finished, and she left for the States. She and Wilding had an agreement; if, after she had received her final decree and he had divorced his current wife, they were still both in favor of it, they would get married.

13

UPON ARRIVAL IN NEW YORK, Elizabeth Taylor stopped at the Hotel Plaza, owned by her former father-in-law, Conrad Hilton. When asked by the management how long she was going to stay, she said five days. She was then ushered to a large and expensive suite and told it was hers without charge, compliments of the management. She was delighted. *This* was a homecoming!

In New York to greet her were her parents, whose twenty-fifth wedding anniversary was almost due. As a result, and because she was spending so much time on the telephone to Michael Wilding in London and expected him to come to the States as soon as he finished the English film he was then at work on, she spent much longer than five days at the Hotel Plaza.

At the end of the month, the hotel presented her their bill. The first five days had been free of charge. From the sixth day onward, she had been paying for a suite far more expensive than one she would have chosen for herself, while under the impression that it was all still on the house.

The bill totaled $2,500.

Outraged, she called Montgomery Clift, who was then living in New York. She had met him originally when they had starred together in *A Place in the Sun,* two years before. They had gotten along famously together from the outset, not so much like brother and sister as like first cousins who had never met until both had grown up, and had then discovered an immediate affinity, a comradeship that had nothing to do with sexual compatibility but which nevertheless had some of the depth and permanence of real love.

It was clear from the outset that Clift was to be her best friend, the one man with whom she could always relax, with whom she could always feel safe. "I've told him everything," she's said, "even things I'm ashamed of."

It was natural for her to think of Montgomery Clift at once when she received the twenty-five-hundred-dollar hotel bill. "I was horrified," she told of it later. "I decided to move and live in one room. I telephoned Monty to come over and help me. We were both so mad we decided to get revenge before leaving. We hung all the pictures upside down, we unscrewed the shower head, we had a flower fight and left stems and petals all over."

In addition, Clift swiped all the towels.

Not long thereafter, Michael Wilding finished the picture on which he'd been working in London and flew to New York where they became engaged, he giving her a sapphire engagement ring surrounded by diamonds.

After a weekend at her Grand-uncle Howard Young's Connecticut estate, the couple flew to California. Elizabeth

Taylor had some final studio scenes of *Ivanhoe* to shoot. She and Wilding stayed in California with Stewart Granger—who was an old friend of Wilding's—and his wife, Jean Simmons.

This was the beginning of an important change in Elizabeth Taylor's social contacts. Until her engagement and marriage to Wilding, she had associated for the most part with other products of the MGM child-star factory; people like Marshall Thompson, Roddy McDowall, Jane Powell, Janet Leigh. Montgomery Clift, with his New York background and more intense attitude toward acting, was in those days virtually unique among her circle of friends.

With the marriage to Wilding, she started associating with a much different group of people. Aside from Stewart Granger and Jean Simmons, the circle expanded to include Richard Burton, Humphrey Bogart and Lauren Bacall, James Mason and his wife Pamela. For the first time, she was going to be in close contact with people who thought acting a serious profession, requiring intellectual preparation, a worthwhile and challenging business for adult minds rather than a precocious technicolor mugging by children of all ages.

Just after the first of the year, 1952, Wilding flew back to England where he had to make another film. He was no sooner gone than Elizabeth Taylor was deluged by well-meaning advice from friends, from studio executives, from casual acquaintances, and from gossip columnists: Stanley Donen had merely been unthinkable for her; Wilding was incredible. She couldn't *really* be planning to marry a man twenty years older than herself?

She could.

The effects of the revolution in Toyland were beginning to make themselves known. It wasn't as easy to intimidate

Elizabeth Taylor as it had been in the days of Bill Pawley. If she had no more rational caution than she had had in those days, she did have more stubbornness. She was going to get married to Michael Wilding whether MGM liked it or not.

She even got Helen Rose, the MGM costume designer who had made her first wedding dress, to design another one for her.

So *there*, MGM!

14

ON FEBRUARY 1, 1952, Elizabeth Taylor received her final decree in her divorce action against Nick Hilton. The same day she officially announced her engagement to Michael Wilding, who was then at work on a movie in England.

Three weeks later Elizabeth Taylor boarded a plane bound for London. For the first time in her life she had successfully fought the studio publicity department's attitude that everything she did was fair game for the flacks of Toyland. That she was going to marry Michael Wilding, the studio knew—and the news had promptly "leaked." Exactly when and where this wedding was to take place only the two families knew, but every journalist who wasn't covering the Korean War was doing his best to find out.

On the London-bound plane, Elizabeth got into an unwary conversation with the passenger beside her. "He was so nice," she explained later, "that I finally told him everything about our wedding. Then, he confided that he'd been planted on the plane by some newspaper to worm all this news out of me . . . but he said he liked me too much to use it now."

If he was telling her the truth—and there's no reason to suppose he wasn't—then the leak came from somewhere else, for there were three thousand uninvited guests on hand for the ceremony, which took place at the Caxton Hall registry office in London on February 21, 1952, six days before her twentieth birthday. Elizabeth Taylor and Michael Wilding were married in a civil ceremony, with only fourteen invited guests, including Wilding's parents, in the registry office.

But there were three thousand unruly fans outside on the sidewalk. And television news cameramen with a Zoomar lens taking films of the ceremony from an office in the building across the street.

The whole affair was so raucous that the newly-married couple were separated by the mob between the registry office door and their car, the new Mrs. Wilding's hat was torn off, and she finally had to be half-carried through the crowd to the car by a London bobby.

After a small reception at Claridge's given by Herbert Wilcox and his wife, Anna Neagle, with the same fourteen guests who had witnessed the wedding, there was an even smaller reception at Wilding's apartment, attended only by his immediate family.

Superficially, this wedding—Elizabeth Taylor's second in twenty-one months and her second before she was out of her teens—was far different from her first venture into marriage.

The first had been a star-studded extravaganza, played for the headlines, whereas both she and Wilding had done their best to make the second wedding a quiet affair. The first had met the enthusiastic approval of family, friends, studio and columnists, while the second was opposed by the studio and the gossip columnists. The first had been marked by hundreds of wedding presents, while the second produced only three wedding gifts, all from friends of Wilding. They included a pair of diamond earrings, a crystal martini shaker and a dictionary. The first had been followed by a five-month honeymoon spent all over Europe, while the second was followed by a one-week honeymoon in the French Alps.

The differences were many, but actually they were superficial. At the first wedding, a gaily childish Elizabeth Taylor had bubbled, "We both love hamburgers with onions, oversized sweaters and Pinza."

Twenty-one months later, with husband number two she said, "For our wedding supper, we ordered pea soup, bacon and eggs, and champagne. The waiter almost dropped dead."

On their fourth anniversary, in 1956, they went to Romanoff's in Beverly Hills and deliberately ordered the same meal.

"When I married him, I had no acting ambition at all—I didn't even want to be an actress. All I wanted at first was to be Mike's wife and to have a baby right away. Where we were to live I left entirely up to him; while I like California better, I could live happily in London or Rome."

It was a brand new world for Elizabeth Taylor, a giddy taste of freedom. For the first time since she was ten years of age, she was not under contract to MGM. Her contract had run out a few months before her second marriage, and she had just been completely uninterested in anything but her husband-to-be.

MGM was not pleased. At last they had managed successfully to bring a child star through adolescence without losing any popularity at all—with, in fact, her popularity increased beyond what it had been—and they had recently discovered, in *A Place in the Sun,* that the kid was not only good box-office but she could act as well. Now, all of a sudden, she was talking like a complete stranger. And her mother couldn't do a thing with her anymore. And, as a topper, her blasted contract had run out!

It was enough to make a studio executive kick his chauffeur.

The boys at MGM tried everything they could think of to get her to sign a new contract. They offered her more money. They tried the personal approach—"Remember the good old days, and the happy gang around the studio?" And they tried to influence her and win her cooperation by giving Michael Wilding a three-year contract.

Nothing worked. Elizabeth just couldn't be bothered.

Finally, after a few months spent living quietly together in Wilding's London flat, the couple suddenly moved back to California, and Elizabeth Taylor signed a new seven-year contract with MGM.

Why? She says, "I re-signed because I got cornball sentimental about Benny Thau and all the other nice people at the studio, and because I thought Michael and I would both be working there and we could have lunch together. But, mainly, it was because I was pregnant. We needed money to get a home of our own—a nest in which to hatch the egg."

Re-signing gave her money. There was no question about that. Her salary was $4,750 per week for forty weeks of the year, for a total annual income of $190,000.

Her first film under the new contract was a pot-boiler, *The Girl Who Had Everything*. That was shot during the summer months of 1952. At the end of August, when the filming was completed, she happily made her announcement at the studio: She was pregnant, and the baby was due January 16th.

The studio promptly suspended her, as per the contract she had so recently signed, meaning she would get only a small portion of her salary until after the baby was born.

In the meantime, Elizabeth and Michael were looking for a house—the nest in which to hatch the egg. It was Wilding who found the place they eventually bought—a sprawling ranch-style house perched on a mountaintop. The price was $75,000, and the place had to be completely redecorated before they could move in.

To help pay for this, Mrs. Wilding cashed all the bonds that had been banked for her under the California state law before she had reached the age of eighteen. They got about $40,000 from that source, and secured the balance of what they needed to buy and redecorate the house—and pay for the baby—by borrowing a frightening amount from MGM, This debt was to be paid back out of Wilding's salary until Elizabeth had the baby and was back at work. After that, it would come out of their joint salaries.

Into Toyland had come another disturbing reality—the laws of money.

15

FOR A WHILE it looked as if this second marriage would really be permanent. Perhaps the solidity and remoteness of the isolated house on the mountaintop helped. Then, too, there were the financial problems which demanded their united attention. And, finally, there were their two children whose well-being was naturally a source of concern to them and whose very presence served to bring Elizabeth and Michael Wilding close together.

Be that as it may, theirs was, nevertheless, a doll house marriage, in which the two of them played at being husband and wife. It was inevitable that sooner or later one of them would get bored with the game.

One of their problems was the fact that, though they were both in the same occupation and employed by the same studio, they never worked together and only once in four years worked simultaneously. In that time, Elizabeth made six films and Wilding made five, and only once were they both working at the same time.

In the fall of 1955, for instance, when Wilding was in Spanish Morocco filming *Zarak Khan* with Anita Ekberg, Elizabeth Taylor managed to spend a month in Morocco with him, between movies of her own. When, in 1954, she lived in England for three months during the shooting of *Beau Brummell,* Wilding could come no closer than Paris. For tax reasons, he couldn't stay with her in London. They were together every weekend in Paris, but during the week she was at work in London and he remained in Paris.

"It was boring for me in Paris. I just drifted about all week," he said later, with a straight face.

Asked about this nomadic existence, in which often as not neither one of them was home, Elizabeth Taylor said, "We don't mind. If one of us is working in Hollywood, then we're together. If one is working abroad, the other goes whenever possible."

Their home itself was a miracle of casual inattention. A reporter who went to interview them in 1956 had this to say, "Most of the Wildings' sheets are ripped, and the grass-cloth wallpaper near the 7-foot-6-inch bed she shares with Michael is shredded by cat claws. Their guests, while eating from a glass-and-teakwood table and drinking vintage wines, find themselves using such mismatched utensils as long-handled iced-tea spoons to pry out grapefruit sections."

Despite their $75,000 house and the $150,000 house plus swimming pool they changed to in 1955, and despite their transatlantic flights to be near one another whenever possible and the aura of wealth that followed them wherever they went, the Wildings were actually in shaky financial condition during the greater part of their marriage. Elizabeth Taylor, for instance, was earning $190,000 a year, but she actually received a tiny fraction of that amount. Income taxes took eighty per cent—around $160,000. Jules Goldstone, her agent, got ten per cent, and her business manager received five per cent. This left about $10,000 a year—a far cry from $190,000.

In addition, there was still the debt to MGM, the money they'd borrowed to buy their first house, which was repaid out of this $10,000 a year. And there was the expense of their household staff which included a cook-housekeeper, a nurse for the babies, a gardener, a relief nurse and relief cook, and Peggy Rutledge—with salaries totaling over $13,000 a year. The expenses were thus in excess of Elizabeth's income and were also taking a good portion of Michael Wilding's studio wages.

With the little money that was left, they had to maintain the aura of romantic wealth necessary to a movie star—America's version of royalty. Automobiles, clothing, jewelry, home—all had to be lavish. When they traveled, it had to be by air. When they were away from home, they had to stay at expensive hotels and occupy only the most luxurious suites.

"We're broke, but we don't care," she said on one occasion. "We get great pleasure out of spending money—so why not enjoy it?"

But one part of the expense was not pleasurable. Thousands of dollars every year were spent on doctor bills and hospital bills, for the older Elizabeth Taylor got, the more frequent and severe became her illnesses and her accidents.

Her first baby, for instance, was due to be born on February 16, 1953. On February 6th, however, when she visited her doctor, Dr. Monrad Aaberg, for a routine checkup, he took X-rays, then told her that she would have to have the child at once, by Caesarean section. She was admitted to the hospital that day, nervous and frightened but joking with her doctors. It was the Santa Monica Hospital, and Dr. Aaberg was joined by the pediatrician, Dr. Milo Brooks.

She was forty-five minutes in the operating room, and was delivered of a seven-pound five-ounce baby boy. Coming back down the hall, she was heard calling, "Michael! Michael! *Michael!*"

Wilding was very nearly as nervous and shaken as she. He ran the full length of the hall to be with her, clasping her hand, as she was wheeled back to her room.

A few months earlier, when she had been suspended for her pregnancy, a friend had said to her, "Do you realize this baby is costing you a hundred fifty thousand dollars?"

"I wouldn't care," she'd replied, "if it cost a million."

It had very nearly cost more than that. It had very nearly cost her life.

A few months later, she was back at work—on a loan-out to Paramount for *Elephant Walk*—when it was accident's turn to take a crack at her. On the last day of filming, a wind machine blew a fragment of steel into her eye. No one realized, at first, what had happened for the simple reason that, though her eye throbbed and pained her, the splinter was too small to be seen. The throbbing continued in her eye for three days until she began to fear she had conjunctivitis. She finally went to her doctor, and he found and removed the steel shard.

A few days later it was discovered that an ulcer had formed on the eye as a result of the bit of steel having been imbedded in the tissue. As a result, she was rushed to the hospital, where just a few months before she had had her first baby, named Michael Howard Wilding. She spent several days there, both eyes bandaged, with the very real possibility that she would lose the sight of her injured eye.

A Hollywood furrier named Teitelbaum got his name in the papers by sending her an ermine eye patch.

Fortunately, the ulcer responded to treatment and no permanent damage to the eye resulted.

16

RICHARD BROOKS, who directed Elizabeth Taylor in such films as *The Last Time I Saw Paris* (1954) and *Cat on a Hot Tin Roof* (1958) once had this to say about her:

"If she opens a beer can, she cuts herself; if there is a chair in the middle of the set, she falls over it while talking over her shoulder to someone."

After the series of misadventures that had already befallen her in her short life, it came as something of a surprise when she gave birth to her second child, on February 27th of 1955 (which is also *her* birthday), with no complications. The boy was named Christopher Edward.

However, this halcyon interlude was only the calm before the storm. Shortly after Christopher was born, his mother went to work on *Giant,* with Rock Hudson and James Dean. She was in and out of the hospital almost from the first day of shooting, and spent nearly as much time in a hospital bed as before the cameras.

The earlier grumblings about some of her vaguer complaints became now out-and-out roars. One person who worked on *Giant* had this to say:

"She would be sitting on the set in a wheel chair, attended by a nurse, because she said she was in such excruciating pain from her sciatic nerve. She would cry when she tried to walk. But at the end of the day's work, she'd yell to Rock Hudson, 'Hey, wait for me!' and she'd run off the set as gaily as if nothing were wrong. Physically, I don't think anything was wrong."

"That's not true," she insisted angrily. "I was really in agony."

Sometime earlier, she had been hospitalized because of a blood clot which had formed behind one knee. She claimed that this was the result of wearing jodhpurs that were too tight for her. She also claimed that she got the sciatic pain because she walked wrong, trying to ease the pressure on the leg with the blood clot.

In normal business procedure, the cast of *Giant* had been insured by the studio, and the insurance company found it had its hands full. Aside from the normal dangers involved in shooting outdoor scenes on a ranch, with live animals and barbed wire and too much sun, there were two very abnormal dangers for the insurance company to worry about. First, there was James Dean, racing around trying to work out the best way to kill himself. Second, there was Elizabeth Taylor, shuttling painfully back and forth between the set and the hospital.

More than once, the insurance company doctor assured her there wasn't a thing wrong with her and that she was just pampering herself. Once she screamed back at him, "Then why do I have this horrible pain?"

Because she really did have it.

The thing was, they were both right. Sciatica, colitis, meningism, twisted colon—these pains have been given any number of respectable names both by Elizabeth Taylor and by her highly-paid medical men, but they all boil down to the same thing:

Sciatica is any form of pain or tenderness of the sciatic nerves in the hip. In other words, what housewives call "nagging backache."

Colitis is an inflammation of the mucous membrane of the colon, which is that part of the large intestine from the caecum to the rectum. In other words, nagging backache.

Meningism is a condition similar to meningitis without inflammation, yet often accompanied by considerable pain. In other words, nagging backache.

Twisted colon is another way of saying *colitis.* In other words, nagging backache.

Nagging backache has never troubled a happy woman. It can often be the result of boredom, of frustration, of dull irritation. It can be a physical nagging at the body which reflects the dull nagging of time at the mind. Many times it is psychosomatic, a nervous disease rather than a physical disease. Yet, it is no less real for this, nor is its pain any less troublesome.

It is easy to discern why Elizabeth Taylor got nagging backache during the last days of her marriage to Nicky Hilton, and just as easy to see why the backache went away the minute handsome Michael Wilding began wining and dining her. But why should she get a backache during the filming of *Giant?*

She had been demanding better films for two years now, ever since she had successfully avoided a dud and been loaned out to Paramount for *Elephant Walk* instead. Now she was getting what she'd been asking for. She had been loaned out to Warner Brothers to play the key role in *Giant*.

It was, up till that time, the toughest acting job of her career, requiring her to essay a wide range of emotional scenes at five different ages. She was playing many of her scenes opposite James Dean, a scenery chewer who had, in his first film, stolen scenes from such stalwarts as Raymond Massey, Julie Harris and Jo Van Fleet. He was now on his third film and loaded for bear. Her other co-star was Rock Hudson, one of the top male stars at the box-office, who had chosen this picture to prove that *he* could act, too.

She was scared. She'd been asking for something she could get her teeth into, and they had handed her a whale. They handed her a *Giant*.

What if she turned out to be a dud? What if everybody else walked off with the picture and left her standing there with her beautiful face hanging out? What if it turned out she was only a good-looking woman after all, and not really an accomplished actress? What if she were making a complete fool of herself, if she were going to have to go back to MGM and admit that she'd been wrong and they'd been right?

If Dean's monolithic intensity was a strong cause of Elizabeth Taylor's self-doubts and nervous illnesses, his attitude of Plutonian indifference to studio moguls, the public, his own skin, and everything else except acting and driving cars at high speed, simultaneously strengthened her and excited her.

For the last five years she had been, for the most part, a passive revolutionary, a person who stood still while the entire world underwent a revolution around her. Her active steps had been few—arguing with the studio once or twice about the films they cast her in, beginning to ignore her husband's advice while striving to make her own decisions—and had resulted in her being cast in this movie which terrified her. It was reassuring to see someone who was so completely an iconoclast, particularly someone like James Dean, who was idolized for just those volatile qualities which had been plucked out of Elizabeth Taylor during her childhood.

During the filming of *Giant,* she gradually made friends with Dean. It was a friendship somewhat like that existing between herself and Montgomery Clift. If the relationship with Clift was like two cousins who'd met after both had grown up, the relationship with Dean was more like two in-laws neither of whom can stand the rest of either family.

Dean's scenes were finished a couple of days before those of the rest of the company. He was excused, and the ban on his driving his Porsche was lifted.

It was the day before the end of the filming. Tomorrow, there would be only one last six-minute scene, in which Elizabeth Taylor played an old woman. On this evening before, the cast was watching the rushes of the day's shooting when the news of Dean's death came to the projection room via telephone, only an hour after it had happened.

Elizabeth Taylor went into hysterics. She stayed at the Warner Brothers studio until after nine in the evening, phoning frantically to the police and to various newspapers, trying to prove that it was a false report, that Dean wasn't really dead.

George Stevens, her director, thought it would be better for her to keep working. There was only the one six-minute scene to do, and he insisted that she come to work the next day, with an eight o'clock makeup call.

Her husband drove her to the studio, and she arrived on time, but she also arrived weeping and disheveled, having not slept at all, crying rebelliously that Stevens was heartless and cold.

Stevens worked patiently with her. By the end of the day she was somewhat calmer and they did have the scene on film, though Stevens admitted, "She didn't play it very well. It was the final scene and I'd wanted to complete the picture. But I knew we'd have to do it over again."

The next day, however, there was no work done on the scene. Instead, Elizabeth Taylor went to the hospital, with what she called a "twisted colon."

Nagging backache.

There was no operation, but she spent two weeks in the hospital before she felt well enough to come out and finish that one last scene. In the meantime, Stevens and the cast and the crew waited for her.

Afterward, she said, "If I hadn't had that blow-up with George Stevens, hysterical and crying, and if I hadn't eaten, it wouldn't have happened."

In *A Place in the Sun,* Elizabeth Taylor had rediscovered something she'd completely forgotten in the six years since *National Velvet;* that acting could be fun and that a screenplay could be a respectable object and not necessarily something whipped together without thought or purpose or direction.

In the same film, MGM rediscovered something *they* had completely forgotten since *National Velvet.* Elizabeth Taylor was not only a beautiful girl—becoming a beautiful woman—she was also a potentially fine actress.

This was in 1951. In 1954, she and the studio had these facts hammered home as a result of *The Last Time I Saw Paris.* And in 1955, the matter was settled once and for all in *Giant.* Her job in this latter film was described in this manner by George Stevens, who had also directed her in *A Place in the Sun:*

"In *Giant,* we gave her a very difficult part: she is the pivot of the whole picture, and she plays five different ages including a grandmother. Beauty of her kind is hard to overcome in characterization—we put a real burden on her shoulders."

Critical praise was virtually unanimous in agreeing that she had carried the burden with ease. But she herself was growing cynical. She told Richard Brooks, who had directed her in *The Last Time I Saw Paris,* "What's the use of my being a good actress? People pay no attention to it, anyway. They just say that, as usual, Elizabeth Taylor looked beautiful."

Brooks told a reporter, "She began to think of her beauty as a handicap, a liability."

During 1954 and 1955, however, a change was taking place in Elizabeth Taylor. She was beginning to realize that she really *could* have a voice in her own affairs, that she *could* make decisions and see them through—that people would give in to her.

When she became pregnant with her second child, in the spring of 1954, she waited as late as possible before informing the studio. She and Wilding were in the process of moving out of their $75,000 mountaintop hideaway into a $150,000 eight-room modern home with swimming pool. "I simply couldn't afford to go on suspension again," she said, "so I gave them another year on my contract."

She was beginning to learn to avoid cornball sentimentality in business deals. She had already decided that she was on her last contract with the studio. After the seven years, she would be a free agent forever.

"With luck," her husband said, "she can earn a million dollars in seven years and be independent the rest of her life."

"With luck," she added, "I can also act only in pictures that interest me. I will never have to do garbage again."

The idea that she could refuse to make a picture on the grounds that she detested it was a new one, and still exciting. She had first tried it shortly after the birth of her first child, in 1953. The studio had promptly suspended her, but she had waited them out—more because she was so interested in her new child and wanted to be with him than because of any sudden stiffening of her backbone. After six weeks they had offered her, instead, the loan out to Paramount for *Elephant Walk*. While not one of the pictures of which she is most proud, *Elephant Walk* was, nevertheless, several cuts above the original bit of fluff she had turned down.

She was also gradually becoming less and less dependent on her husband. During the first two years of their marriage, he made all the decisions; it was her role merely to applaud them. He chose California as the place where they would live, he chose the house and its furnishings, and he was the one who decided to make the move to the new house two years later.

This, too, was changing, and it was partly as a result of the new friends she had come to know as the wife of Michael Wilding. Until then she had been the shyest of wall-flowers at parties she attended. Indeed, this had been one of the problems during the dateless years of her teens. But Wilding's friends prodded her out of her shell.

"I used to watch, observe, overhear conversations, and make my own comments to myself, some cynical," she has said. "I was never bored, but neither did I mix. Then, when I married Michael, I couldn't detach myself from his apron strings; I'd follow him from group to group like a puppy dog."

The people around her didn't care for the puppy dog routine, and once or twice she was told about it. One time, at a party at the home of Charles Vidor, she came out of the powder room, saw Humphrey Bogart, and immediately asked her inevitable question, "Where's Michael?"

Bogart glowered for a second, then took her to one side, saying, "Let me talk to you, kid. It's damned stupid for you to keep following your husband around. You should be asserting yourself. Be something in your own right; stop being a shadow."

One or two lectures like that, from people she respected both as individuals and as actors, was enough to set her thinking. What with her friends urging her to stand on her own two feet, and what with the critics agreeing that in such films as *A Place in the Sun* and *The Last Time I Saw Paris* she was emerging as a really fine actress, and what with her studio backing down when she refused to make a particular film, it was inevitable that she would begin to explore her own resources, push her freedom of choice as far as she could to find out just how much of a free agent she was.

In an interview in 1956, she said, "Don't ask *me* about *acting*. But some day, I think I will be an actress. I'm now learning and developing; I'm trying . . . I've always been an instinctive actress as opposed to an instructed one. I have no technique. I just try to *become* the other person. Some people act by charts—or by the Stanislavski method. I can only do it by forgetting myself completely, even moving or picking up things by impulse."

An *instinctive* actress. She described herself perfectly, in an apologetic and unassuming manner, not realizing when she spoke that actors who use charts or methods—techniques of any kind at all—are simply trying to train themselves to do what she could do naturally.

But by 1956, she was at least sure of herself sufficiently to say, "I'll never be afraid of suspension again; never again will I play a part in which I don't believe."

And Wilding, plaintive, watching the child-bride he'd married grow away from him, told her, "The happiest years of my marriage were when you were so dependent on me . . . I hate it now. Now, I follow you around. Now, I'm left alone in a corner."

No one knows exactly when it started. It became noticeable, however, in November of 1955, when *Confidential* magazine, then at the peak of its power and determined to leave no stone unthrown, cast a beady eye on Michael Wilding and came up with a story cumbersomely entitled,

"When The Cat's Away, The Mike Will Play—Even When It's Liz Taylor's Hubby!"

The article was as unlikely as its title. It told a completely bizarre story about Michael Wilding, another man, a photographer, and two strip-teasers, one of them self-titled "The Bazoom Girl." According to *Confidential's* unimpeachable authority, after Elizabeth Taylor had gone to Texas in June of 1955 to film the location shots of *Giant,* Michael Wilding had hied himself to a strip joint in a less desirable section of Los Angeles, with a male friend, and while there picked up the two strippers and the photographer. One of these strippers was a movie actress herself, as it turned out; she was to do a strip for the camera the following day. Not the MGM camera, exactly—it was a camera owned by a man with a mail order business.

Wilding, according to the story, left the nightclub with the other four and took them all to his place for a snack. The movie-type stripper then donned her gauze and rehearsed a while by the pool. Wilding and the other two men, the story insisted, watched these gyrations through a window, from inside the garage!

From here on, the story—told in the insistently-Broadwayese style of *Confidential*—gets just a little incomprehensible. The photographer drifted away at some point, and so did The Bazoom Girl, and so did the other male. This left Wilding in the garage and the movie star out by the pool. Finishing her calisthenics, this prize winner went on into the house and wandered around a bit. Wilding left the garage to trail her. When she went into his wife's bedroom he told her it was his wife's bedroom and she had to come back out again.

So she got miffed and went home.

That, more or less, was the story. It was probably the most oblique example of sexuality since the panty-raid, but there it was in *Confidential.* There was no suggestion or implication that Wilding had had carnal knowledge of either of the strippers, or even that he had had any such designs on them.

To believe the literal truth of the story was not to believe that Michael Wilding had been unfaithful to Elizabeth Taylor. It was only to believe that Michael Wilding was unhinged.

But Toyland has its own way of looking at things. Speaking of it later, Elizabeth Taylor said, "By the time the magazine came out, I was back home in Hollywood. Neither Michael nor I knew about the article until it had been on the newsstands for three days. Then a columnist telephoned poor Michael at home to know how I'd acted about it. Horrified, Mike rushed out and bought the magazine. Then he telephoned me on the set. He was absolutely aghast, and his voice was so pale gray that I couldn't help giggling."

She was giggling, but she was the only one. An MGM executive, who had been working with her on *Giant,* offered to get her a bachelor-girl apartment at the studio. She could now live in Toyland all day and all night, forever and ever. She looked at him in blank astonishment and said, "You mean you want me to leave my home, my husband and my children?"

He had had something like that in mind, yes.

"Whether it's true or not," she said later, "you can't let an article like that break up your marriage."

Yet, just about a year later, the marriage did break up. If it wasn't the article in *Confidential* that had done the trick—and it wasn't—then what had?

"We don't pick and quarrel, but we do fight—it's garbage to say we don't," she said, a few months before they separated. "Until a year ago, we didn't; we always counted ten. But I think it's healthy to blow your lid now and then. What infuriates me about Michael is that he can be so underplaying. My temper is Irish, and when I blow, I blow."

What did they argue about? Basically, about the new Elizabeth Taylor, the one who no longer welcomed Michael Wilding's guidance and advice so completely and wholeheartedly. And where the difference in their age had never mattered before—when she was perfectly content to be as young as possible at all times and leave the problems to the grown-ups—the twenty years between their birthdays loomed large when she began to assert her own will and independence.

Wilding was too used to his child-bride accepting his every suggestion as Revelation. When she started talking back it was humanly impossible not to remind her that he was twenty years older than she and, therefore, by simple seniority, wiser in the ways of the world. To which she once answered, angrily, "If you tell me black is red, I won't believe you, regardless of your age; but if you can give me a good story, I will . . . I'm not your daughter, I'm your wife."

Another time, she was quoted as having cried, in the heat of battle, "Don't treat me like a baby! I'm your *wife!*"

Unfortunately, it wasn't possible for Wilding to see it that way and retain his self-respect. As long as he was a paternal guardian and trusted advisor, it didn't matter so much that she was the major breadwinner in the family. But when he was only a husband, he wasn't even that, he was only a kept boy and he didn't like it. At first, he was plaintive, "underplaying," as his wife had said. But gradually he got more irritated, and their arguments became more violent. Finally there were practically no safe subjects between them any more.

"After a while, we had nothing to talk about but what happened at the studio that day," she said.

On October 3, 1956, the announcement was made. They were separated, and she would sue for divorce on the grounds of mental cruelty. She wanted no alimony, asking only $250 a month for support of their children. On November 14th of 1956, the divorce was granted, at Santa Monica, California. Shortly thereafter Wilding remarried and moved back to London.

Said Elizabeth Taylor: "I know of only a few marriages that are happy when a wife is a star."

BOOK IV

Pegasus

17

ONE TIME SHE WAS IN KENTUCKY, and he invited her to lunch. She accepted the invitation, and he took her to lunch—in Chicago. The tab came to a thousand dollars, but that was all right; he was courting her.

She was Elizabeth Taylor, fresh from her divorce of Michael Wilding. *He* was Mike Todd, the P. T. Barnum of the Twentieth Century, and made of solid brass. *He* had decided he was going to marry *her*, and there wasn't a damn thing she could do to avoid it. Into Toyland had come barging a mad capering creature with some of the qualities of a bugle and some of the qualities of a Sherman tank.

He was born Avrom Hirsch Goldbogen in Minneapolis, Minnesota, sometime in the first decade of the century. He swore the birth date was June 22, 1909; his brother insisted it was actually in December of 1908. Other members of the family thought they were both wrong.

In any case, it didn't take him long to get moving and show the stuff he was made of. At the age of five, he went to work as an assistant to a pushcart peddler. At seven, he graduated to newspaper delivery, and the same year he became involved for the first time with show business, playing cornet in a boys' band and working the carnivals that came to town. When school threatened to take up valuable time that could be spent hustling a buck, he became banker of a floating crap game for the rest of the student body. By this time, the family had moved from Minneapolis to Chicago, but by this time Mike was *ready* for Chicago.

At the age of fifteen he talked a trade school into installing a bricklaying course, and he and the school split the tuition. At the same time, he was honing his producing and promotional talents by throwing "lost-our-lease sales" for small merchants around town.

A year later, he became a real estate operator and a builder, and before he was twenty he'd made his first million. He promptly lost it—still before he was twenty—when the bond house backing his company went bankrupt.

"I've been broke," he once said, "but I've never been poor. Being poor is a state of mind; being broke is only a temporary situation."

At seventeen, he had married a Chicago girl named Bertha Freshman. Once his first million was gone, he and Bertha moved out to Hollywood to get another one. He started a corporation that soundproofed movie stages.

In 1929, when he was twenty, his son was born and was given the name of Michael Goldbogen. He decided about the same time to change his name. Since, as an infant, he had mispronounced "coat" as "toat," his nickname had been "Toat" among members of the family ever since. He changed Toat to Todd, and borrowed his son's first name, thereby becoming Mike Todd.

In 1933, he returned to Chicago to launch his first production in show business at the Chicago World's Fair. The attraction he promoted was called a "Flame Dance." It involved a dancer dressed as a moth, whose costume was gradually singed off during the number.

From this modest opening salvo, Mike Todd hurried on to bigger and better things. He roared into New York, proclaiming himself a Broadway producer, and pogo-sticked over his first two shows—*Call Me Ziggy* and *The Man from Cairo*—both flops—with hardly a backward glance. His next show was a smash—*The Hot Mikado,* a jazz version of the Gilbert & Sullivan operetta, starring Bill "Bojangles" Robinson.

After *Peep Show,* he promulgated his theatrical credo: "I believe in giving the customers a meat and potatoes show. Dames and comedy—high dames and low comedy, that's my message."

Another time, he said of his life as a Broadway producer, "It's a hard way to make an easy living."

Joe E. Lewis described him: "He definitely belongs on a runaway horse."

All in all, he produced twenty-one Broadway shows. Some hit and some missed; and some hit that should have missed only because of Todd's clever and brassy showmanship.

It was in 1945, with *Up in Central Park,* that he first tried throwing a mammoth party as a publicity stunt. The entire first night audience was invited to a party after the show—up in Central Park. They rode up in hansom cabs, in broughams, in barouches and victorias and tallyhos, arriving to find a champagne and caviar party at the Tavern on the Green.

His first wife died in 1946. A year later he married Joan Blondell, a match that lasted three years. They were divorced in 1950, and it was seven years before he married again.

Through the years he made and lost millions. Huge sums of money were gambled away at the race track or at the poker table. As recently as 1947, he had been involved in bankruptcy proceedings, owing more than a million dollars to one hundred sixteen creditors.

He was one of the founders of the company that produced Cinerama, sold out and went to work on Todd-AO. The first film in Todd-AO, *Oklahoma,* had barely opened in 1955 when Todd sold that, too, and invested every penny he could lay his hands on in *Around the World in Eighty Days.* It cost him six-and-a-half million dollars, and in less than two years had grossed five times that amount.

He was a short, stocky, dark-haired man with bunched shoulders and a harried expression. His speech was staccato, his movements the prowling of a chunky cat. He was a slave to the telephone, and for years had two in his bedroom, two in the living room, and two in his penthouse terrace, all with twenty-foot extension cords so he could pace up and down while talking. The phones were in pairs because one was a direct line to his office and the other was an outside line with an unlisted number.

He felt nervous unless he had a telephone in one hand and a cigar in the other. He promoted his enterprises and himself with equal fervor, with complete self-confidence and with an absolute lack of embarrassment.

Before Elizabeth Taylor was born, he had already made and lost his first million.

When *she* was born, *he* had a two-year-old son.

When *she* was just starting with Universal, *he* was running a revue at the New York World's Fair starring Gypsy Rose Lee.

When *she* was at the awkward age and writing *Nibbles and Me, he* was throwing a party for a whole first-night audience, in Central Park.

When *she* was getting her first screen kiss in *Cynthia, he* was going bankrupt again, in a New York court.

When *she* was divorcing Michael Wilding, *he* was beginning to rake in the returns on *Around the World in Eighty Days* and looking around for new worlds to conquer.

He saw *her.*

He started courting her, in a manner that Phineas Fogg would have thoroughly approved. He showered her with paintings, jewels, furs—luncheons in Chicago. It was raucous, it was wild and woolly, it was as romantic as a five-pound firecracker, but it worked.

The thing was, Mike Todd looked at Elizabeth Taylor and saw a queen. There's no doubt of it. She was The Queen, and he was a whole country full of loyal subjects rolled up in one. The steady stream of expensive presents, which in any other man would have been only boorish, was with Mike Todd simply the expression of homage, and they both realized it.

People had always looked upon Elizabeth Taylor as a queen. The movie studio saw her as a queen and themselves as the palace guard and cabinet of ministers. Her first two husbands had regarded her as a queen and themselves as prime consorts. Her mother and her fans had seen *themselves* as queens, through her.

Mike Todd was something else again. He worshipped her as a queen should be worshipped, and at the same time he controlled her as all modern monarchs are controlled by their subjects. A very bright man who had managed to get through his public school education with virtually none of it having rubbed off on him, he was to a great extent self-educated, with a broad range of knowledge in a fantastic variety of fields.

Joseph Mankiewicz, who would later direct Elizabeth Taylor in *Suddenly, Last Summer,* once said, "More than anyone realizes, Mike was responsible for the intellectual and emotional awakening of this girl. For all his flamboyance, he was a man of an infinite variety of interests. Through him, Elizabeth became the step-grandmother of three children. She also traveled widely, meeting world statesmen and artists, swindlers and scientists, bankers and racket chiefs. Before that, she had been a sort of a Sleeping Beauty in an isolated castle. Mike took her through the cobwebs to the outer world, in which there is something more than movie producers and wardrobe women. Before Todd, the people she knew outside the motion picture industry could probably be counted on the fingers of one hand."

At long last, the ivory ghetto had crumbled. This hoarse-voiced gargoyle had come rampaging in, pulling down the pink curtains around Toyland, and the world came tumbling in behind him.

18

ON DECEMBER 8, 1956, having finished *Raintree County,* Elizabeth Taylor went into the hospital for a five-hour operation, the result of a crushed spinal disc. There was a long recovery period necessary—nearly two months—and when she came out Mike Todd was waiting for her with a present:

A thirty-carat engagement ring!

It was the culmination of an incredibly short and noisy courtship, and Mike Todd, true to his quick, impatient character, wanted the marriage to take place right away. But it was only the end of January, and the final decree in the divorce from Wilding wouldn't be coming through until the middle of November.

The hell with that! Todd couldn't twiddle his thumbs for ten months. He had work to do.

So he and Elizabeth went to Mexico and got a divorce that didn't have a lot of strings attached to it. That was on January 31, 1957. The same day they announced their engagement, and Todd reached for two or three phones to promote himself a wedding.

It was a Mike Todd sort of wedding—big and loud and flashy and not in the best taste in the world. But Todd had a *flair* for bad taste; he did the most boorish things in the world with such a mad air of harried nonchalance that the bad taste didn't really matter any more. Wherever Mike Todd was, the Mad Hatter's tea party could not be far away.

On February 2, 1957, two days after the Mexican divorce, the wedding took place—in Acapulco.

The Mayor of Acapulco officiated.

The whole damn city was invited to the reception.

It was a festival to rival a Saint's Day—the kind of thing a traveloguist would give his left arm for.

After the wedding and the festival and all the confetti, they flew to a hospital in New York where she had been operated on two months earlier. Her back was acting up again and she stayed long enough to take some treatments, and then the two of them were off again.

Where to?

Where else? A world tour.

On August 7, 1957, the world tour was delayed temporarily so that Elizabeth Taylor could give birth to her third child and first daughter. The infant was named Elizabeth Francis—for her mother and grandfather—and deposited in the nursery with her half-brothers, Michael and Christopher, while her mother and father went back on the world tour.

The delivery had been a difficult and dangerous one—more difficult and dangerous than the birth of her first child—which was only to be expected with Elizabeth Taylor.

Her happiness, her achievements, her wealth, all were greater than they ever had been. It was inevitable that her pains and illnesses would be equivalently greater.

The world tour faltered a second time, this time for good, in Hong Kong, on November 16th of 1957, when Elizabeth Taylor was admitted to a hospital with what was described as a "slight case" of appendicitis.

Two days later Mike Todd canceled the planned rest of the tour, and brought his wife back to the United States, to the Cedars of Lebanon Hospital in Los Angeles, where, on December 17th, she had an appendectomy.

She was soon up and doing again, and on January 15, 1958, she and her husband left New York for Moscow where Todd was to give a special performance of *Around the World in Eighty Days.* The trip was a leisurely one, and they arrived in Moscow ten days later, on the 25th. On the 27th, they attended a diplomatic reception at the Indian Embassy in Moscow in honor of India's National Day. Among those present were the ambassadors of Britain, France, Canada, Italy and Norway, and Nikita Khrushchev.

They stayed a little more than a week, then returned to California. Elizabeth Taylor was starting her first motion picture in more than a year—*Cat on a Hot Tin Roof.* She was also a contender for the Academy Award to be presented two months later, for her role in *Raintree County,* in which she starred opposite her old friend, Montgomery Clift.

The first wedding anniversary of Mike Todd and Elizabeth Taylor, February 2, 1958, came when they were both in California. She was starting *Cat,* and he was in the process of overseeing the scripting of his second motion picture, *Don Quixote.*

The first year had been a gas. Elizabeth Taylor had ignored everything—the demands of the studio, the existence of her profession—and had immersed herself in Mike Todd's peripatetic way of life. She had been hospitalized twice, once for an appendectomy and once to have her third child, but these hospitalizations had been far different from many of her hospitalizations in the past. There was no noisy self-pity, no loud oft-repeated protestations that she really *was* sick, no long drawn-out recuperations. She went into the hospital at the last possible minute, came out again at the first opportunity, and went bouncing off with her volatile, travel-prone husband.

Four months earlier, Todd had let the whole world know that he thought his wife a queen, when he threw his famous (or infamous) *Around the World in Eighty Days* party on October 17, 1957, at Madison Square Garden. The party celebrated the first anniversary of the opening of the movie—it was Todd's first, and he'd won an Academy Award for it—and was probably the most grandiose example of personal publicity by a non-political figure in the history of the world.

There were eighteen thousand guests, and the attractions included Sir Cedric Hardwick riding an elephant and Fernandel leading a horse around the ring, with comic and horse wearing identical expressions of gloom. (The party was just a bit too big; it got out of control and became simply a melee: Those down front got drunk, and those in back shared Hershey bars.)

At any rate, the high point of the party—ninety minutes of which was televised by CBS—was Mike Todd's presentation of his wife to his guests, a presentation that involved bands playing solemn marches, a cake of unbelievable size, and in general all the paraphernalia for a sort of borscht circuit coronation.

It would have been funny, except that he so obviously meant it. Elizabeth was a queen, *his* queen, and nothing was too good for her.

At the same time, she was a modern queen and he was like a modern nation full of loyal subjects. That is, he worshipped her and he insisted on running her life. In so doing, he began with the assumption that she had a life worth running. She realized this, commenting once, "It's nice to be married to someone who thinks I have a brain."

"She doesn't want to work," he said of her, "and wants to be bossed."

To which she purred proudly, "At last, I've got a real man."

Although travel was by no means a new experience to Elizabeth Taylor—she had been to England any number of times while making movies, and had traveled to such out-of-the-way locations as Spanish Morocco when accompanying Michael Wilding on *his* film-making—she had never run across anything like Mike Todd before. He was constantly on the go, once traveling to Europe three times in three weeks. She stayed with him, doggedly at first and then with more and more enjoyment, saying, "When we're separated, we die. So it's easier for me to pick up and travel with Mike."

In that first year of marriage, from February 2, 1957 in Mexico, to February 2, 1958 in Hollywood, Mike Todd showed Elizabeth Taylor the vast, wide world outside Toyland, and she looked at it all in fascination. He gave her a cram course of knowledge and experience which she could never have obtained so long as she remained in Toyland.

He set a breakneck pace, and she kept up with him. By the end of the first year, when they were in Hollywood and she had just started back to work, it was clear that what had originally looked like an incredibly mismatched marriage was going to work out, and that both parties were gaining thereby. Mike Todd was gradually learning how to slow down from time to time, and Elizabeth Taylor was finding her real self.

When she went to work in *Cat on a Hot Tin Roof,* he moved his office to the MGM lot so he could be near her and watch her progress. He stopped by the set every day and looked at the rushes with her every evening. "You've never been so good in your life," he told her. "Maybe you won't win the Academy Award for *Raintree County,* but you'll win it next year for this one."

And then he was off in search of a telephone. Or planning a lightning trip to New York over the weekend.

"One of these days," she said. "I will be too old for him."

19

FORTY-EIGHT DAYS after their first wedding anniversary, Mike Todd was dead.

He was headed east in his private plane, the *Lucky Liz,* with a writer named Art Cohn and a crew consisting of pilot and co-pilot. It was one of the very few times since he'd married Elizabeth Taylor that she wasn't with him—she had the flu and was home in bed with a temperature of 102 degrees.

The plane went down in the Zuni Mountains, ninety miles west of Albuquerque in rugged isolated country. There were no survivors.

When Elizabeth heard about it, she refused to believe it. Three years before, she had spent hours trying to disprove the report of James Dean's death, and her hysterical reaction at that time was nothing to her reaction when she was told that Mike Todd was dead.

She jumped up from bed and ran out of the room, her hands to her ears. Her doctor, her secretary, her friends, followed her around the house, trying to get her to calm down, but she would let none of them near her.

If they tried to talk to her, she would scream, not in grief or pain but to drown out what they were saying. She refused to acknowledge that he was dead. She dodged and dashed and careened about their house, nightgowned, her hair streaming, her face twisted in grief. And all the while her friends pursued her, soft-voiced, their hands out to her, seeking in vain to bring her some solace from pain and sorrow.

A friend said later, "If it wasn't that she thought of the children, she would have killed herself, she surely would."

She could only run for so long, she could only blot out the truth for so long. Eventually, she collapsed, absolutely spent, and they carried her back to her bed. Her physician, Dr. Rexford Kennemar, and her brother Howard stayed with her.

Two days later, Howard and Dr. Kennemar flanked her, supporting her as she left the house for the long journey to Chicago where her husband was to be buried. On March 25th he was interred. The funeral was marred by a squabble among his brothers. Immediately afterward Elizabeth went back to California.

On the third try, she had found the man, had finally found the right man. She was not the beautiful life-size doll to be seen with, that Nicky Hilton had apparently been looking for. She was not the glamorous, completely dependent female that Michael Wilding had apparently held as his ideal. She was not a creation of Toyland.

She was a woman. And she had finally found the right man. And he had just started to help her find herself.

A brazen buffoon, an accomplished conman, a purveyor to lowbrows, a loud-mouthed peasant—Mike Todd was all of those. He was also a quiet listener, a generous friend, a tasteful patron of the arts, a brilliant showman . . .

. . . And the right man for Elizabeth Taylor.

Elizabeth went back to work on *Cat on a Hot Tin Roof* three weeks after Mike Todd's death. In that time she had lost eight pounds, had eaten no solid food at all, and had developed a slight stammer which continued off screen for several weeks.

The film's director, Richard Brooks, said, "It was rough. I didn't see her eat a thing for about twenty days."

Lawrence Weingarten, producer of the picture, said, "She was so weak from lack of food that she couldn't lift a suitcase off a bed in the first scene she played."

The first time she ate any sort of a real meal was when they were shooting Big Daddy's birthday party scene. Ham, vegetables and sour-dough bread were on the table, and she wolfed it down so hungrily that Brooks ran through extra takes of the scene just to get food into her.

"The only reason I want to do it is because of Mike," she said, explaining her return to the film. "Mike liked me in this picture and I want to finish it for him."

"The work helped her keep her mind off her tragedy," said Brooks. "Then I noticed something new and wonderful in her acting. In throwing herself into her work to ease her pain, she was beginning to make full use of the great instrument of her talent for the first time—something she'd never seemed to care about before."

"She was remarkable," said Weingarten. "She was working on a string for the first two weeks after her return, but you can't see a flaw in her performance."

The first time they came to the scene where the grandchildren sing *For He's A Jolly Good Fellow* to Big Daddy, who doesn't know that he is mortally ill, she burst into tears. "I just couldn't stop thinking about that poor man standing there, dying of cancer and not knowing it," she said.

After a break, when they were about to do the scene again, she said to Brooks, "How am I going to do this scene? I'll start to cry as soon as I have to start talking about death."

"*Use* it," he told her. "*Use* what's happening to you here."

Afterwards, he said, "She was like a strong, young fastball pitcher in baseball who had just learned to mix his natural speed with a curve that would break in an exact spot over the plate. She was absolutely great—and she won an Academy Award nomination."

Burl Ives, who'd already played Big Daddy opposite three other actresses on the stage, said it all much more succinctly:

"She's the best of the bunch."

"Since Mike Todd's death," said Richard Brooks, shortly after he'd finished directing her in *Cat,* "Elizabeth has begun to study herself as a human being and an artist. She wants to work, not because she is lonely or needs money, but because it is what he would have wanted her to do."

"Mike's legacy to me," she said once, "was the way he opened my eyes to new people and things, the way he taught me to use my curiosity and to ask 'Why?' I used to be terribly shy and ashamed to show my ignorance when I didn't understand something. Now I stand right up there and ask questions and try to learn about things and people and what they are and why they are."

Todd had showed her, at last, that there was more to the world than the gingerbread vistas of Toyland, but he had died before she had more than barely begun to make the adjustment from perennial child to woman. After his death, the adjustment came quickly and abruptly.

"What brought it about," said Brooks, "was life, pain, the necessity to work under adverse conditions as an artist and a woman, after years of an incredibly sheltered existence."

A month after Todd's death, his will was probated. He left a one-million-dollar estate, including one hundred percent of *Around the World in Eighty Days.* Half of this empire went to his son, Michael Todd, Jr. The other half he left to Elizabeth Taylor.

She was now a business woman, whether she liked it or not. The days of sloppy financial thinking—when she could borrow years ahead on her MGM salary to move out of a $75,000 house she'd remodeled two years before into a $150,000 house that she needed no more than she could afford—were, of necessity, behind her. She was surrounded by business advisors, the associates of her husband, but ultimate decision was in her hands. And the decisions involved more serious problems and considerations than whether she should take a suspension for her pregnancy or give the studio another year on her contract.

On the set, she used the death of her husband to give depth and reality to her acting. Away from the set, the lawyers and businessmen of Michael Todd Co., Incorporated, urged her to use the death of her husband for tax purposes, and, in essence, she sued herself for negligence in Mike Todd's death. That is, on August 21, 1958, she sued Michael Todd Co., Incorporated, the lessee of the plane, plus Ayer Lease Plan, Inc. and Trade-Ayer, Inc., for a total of five million dollars.

It was not, they assured her, a sign of disrespect to the memory of her husband. It was a sound business move, and no one would approve a sound business move faster than Mike Todd. That made sense. Nevertheless, it was a while before she agreed.

Time blunts pain. The use of pain, its redirection in the task of acting, blunts it faster. The use of its cause as a sound business move blunts it even faster.

In the meantime, she wandered. "I don't do TV or stage work," she said, "so I'll have to stay somewhere near Hollywood. I want to keep on working. I'm reading scripts constantly, looking for something to do."

Her contract with MGM was drawing to a close. The last slender thread that still connected her to Toyland was slowly unraveling.

Five months after Todd's death she told a friend, "I'm at a point where I want to make up my own mind and decide things for myself, even if I'm wrong."

The friend said of this statement, "It was obvious that she was now in open revolt."

But it wasn't obvious, not really. It would get *really* obvious in just a week or two.

BOOK V

Let's All Hate Liz

20

"WHAT MOST PEOPLE DON'T KNOW is that there has been a smoldering spirit of revolt in Elizabeth for a long time. I sometimes wonder if she didn't unconsciously provoke the Debbie-Eddie mess deliberately, because, in growing up, she finally had to give violent expression to her revolt."

The speaker is George Stevens who directed Elizabeth Taylor in *A Place in the Sun* and *Giant.*

"The facts seem to me to prove she has been aggressive in her romances, ruthless in her disregard for the feelings of those who have stood in her path and indifferent to the wreckage she has left behind her."

The speaker is Elsa Maxwell.

Time, Life and *Newsweek* all headlined it in their issues for September 22, 1958. Of the three, *Life's* peculiar form of reportage took the prize, with a headline that read: TALE OF DEBBIE, EDDIE AND THE WIDOW TODD.

The tale itself was almost as good as the one *Confidential* had run three years earlier on Michael Wilding. Eddie Fisher, then married to Debbie Reynolds, had two weeks earlier been in New York, and so had Elizabeth Taylor. They'd known each other for years—Debbie, in fact, had cared for Elizabeth Taylor's children after Mike Todd died—and they had, during the past two weeks in New York, gotten to know one another better than ever.

Broadway columnist Earl Wilson giggled to his readers that "Liz and Eddie" had been "dancing it up" at various nightclubs around town. And the next thing anybody knew, they had spent a simultaneous weekend at Grossinger's over Labor Day.

Life, as happy as a returning U-2 pilot, displayed photographs showing Liz and Eddie leaving the Blue Angel, a New York nightclub, separately, and then meeting again in the back seat of a Cadillac, said back seat also occupied by Eva Marie Saint.

At first, everybody denied everything. Elizabeth Taylor said, "I don't know what it's all about." Eddie, in an article written for the Chester, Pennsylvania *Times,* wrote that he was "willing to do anything to save our marriage . . . As for Liz and I being in love, it is utter nonsense." Debbie didn't say anything at all—at the time.

In a matter of days the whole country was in an uproar. It was almost as though everyone had bet real money on the permanence of the Fisher-Reynolds marriage, and they'd all bet the wrong way. People who'd never met any of the three were highly incensed, and calling all three by their first names. (In the main branch of the Brooklyn Public Library, every color photograph of Elizabeth Taylor printed in every magazine owned by the library was ripped out and spirited away. Whether this was done in an excess of love or hate the librarians have never been able to figure out.)

When Eddie got home, he found out Debbie had been keeping up with the news of the world. While a group of newsmen lived the soft life on the Fisher front lawn, Debbie and Eddie roamed about inside, arguing strenuously. At one point, Debbie was quoted as shouting, "What's the matter with you, anyway?"

After a while, Eddie came out, looking distracted, and joined the lawn-loungers. "Debbie and I are having a misunderstanding," he explained. "Married people do have arguments and misunderstandings."

Then he went back inside for another round.

Pretty soon, Debbie came out. She felt like talking to the people on the lawn, too. "It seems unbelievable to say you can live happily with a man and not know he doesn't love you," she told them.

After another little while, both of them came out. This time, however, they didn't stop to chat with the news hawks. They jumped over a garden wall, dove into a waiting car, and were whisked away to get a little privacy.

Throughout the whole thing, just to give it the properly unrealistic Toyland effect, press agents comforted the reporters with hamburgers and ice cream.

Meanwhile, Elizabeth Taylor had gone home from the airport, where she'd insisted that she didn't know what it was all about, and thought it over. When Hedda Hopper phoned her, she decided she did know what it was all about after all, and that she might just as well start talking:

"You can't break up a happy marriage," she said, citing a truism that was to be completely overlooked in the days ahead. "He's not in love with her and never has been," she added, which was pretty much what Debbie was saying to the lawn brigade at just around the same time. "Only a year ago, they were about to get a divorce but stopped it when they found out she was going to have another baby."

Miss Hopper asked Elizabeth Taylor what she thought Mike Todd's reaction to the current hassle would be, and got the reply, "Mike is dead and I'm alive."

Aside from the fact that that is a statement which could be spoken with any one of half a dozen inflections, implying half a dozen different meanings, none of them as brutal as that implied by the words uninflected in cold print, it is still a pretty harsh comment from a woman who'd been a widow only six months, and who had loved her husband as strongly and completely as Elizabeth Taylor so obviously had.

Why in the world would she say such a thing?

To this day she still wears the thirty-carat $92,000 engagement ring Todd gave her in January of 1957. A huge photograph of him dominates her living room.

Regardless of this, she had at the time of the statement been a motion picture actress for eighteen years. She knew what publicity was, and she knew the difference between good publicity and bad publicity. And she certainly knew that Hedda Hopper intended to print whatever she said.

So why did she say it?

There is a distinct choice of reasons, outlined in two statements at the beginning of this chapter. One of the two almost certainly must be right.

Maybe George Stevens is right. Or maybe Elsa Maxwell is right.

Life goes on, and once Eddie and Debbie had separated and Debbie had announced that she was suing for a divorce, things quieted down a lot. They quieted so much that less than a month later *Look,* which had ignored the whole thing up to this point, carried a feature on Elizabeth Taylor's role of Maggie in *Cat on a Hot Tin Roof* which also included some speculation as to her future marriage plans, giving Eddie Fisher a low second-place on the "possible" list, after Arthur Loew, Jr., the film mogul. The article went on to state, "The consensus is that she will remarry, and that she will follow the pattern of choosing a husband who is rich, handsome, masculine and considerably older than she is."

This was not the first rumor linking Elizabeth Taylor and Arthur Loew. At one party which both attended, they played on the rumors a bit. During a lull in conversation, Loew leaned toward her and stage-whispered, "Shall I tell them, or do you want to?"

She smiled, blushed prettily, looked coy, and whispered back, "You tell them."

The whispers had been loud enough so that this exchange got the attention of everyone else hi the room. Loew then turned and told them:

"Dinner is served."

During this time, she was still drifting. She had completed *Cat,* the film she had finished primarily as therapy after Mike Todd had died, and after that she had done nothing at all. She visited friends—staying with Arthur Loew's sister in Tucson, Arizona, and with Stewart Granger and Jean

Simmons at their place in California— and seemed to be waiting to see what the results of her revolt would be.

The results, for the most part, could have readily been predicted. The gossip columnists—who had written tons of soggy verbiage on the Eddie-Debbie "perfect" marriage (America's Sweethearts), and so felt a proprietary interest in it—turned against her en masse, discovering that she'd been a stinker for years, ever since she'd maltreated poor Nicky Hilton. The newspapers and general magazines made big snide splashes for a little while, and then lost interest, going on to newer and fresher news. The studio was terrified of the bad publicity, but was too terrified of her—less than two years left on the contract—to complain overly much. The friends she wanted to keep, she kept.

Within a month or two the revolt had petered out, as it was bound to do. For she wasn't revolting against Debbie Reynolds, nor was she revolting against Elsa Maxwell and Hedda Hopper, nor was she revolting against George Stevens or Richard Brooks, nor was she revolting against motion pictures such as *Raintree County* and *Cat on a Hot Tin Roof.*

She was revolting against the past. She was revolting against *Love Is Better Than Ever* and *The Courage of Lassie.* She was revolting against the Toyland from which Mike Todd had already freed her. She was revolting against the ivory ghetto that Mike Todd had already torn down.

You can't revolt against the past, at least not for long. It doesn't resist, it doesn't fight back. You turn away from it, you make changes, you renounce it, but you don't engage in a full-scale revolution against it.

That was what Elizabeth Taylor was trying to do, and it didn't work. It fizzled. When a revolutionary gets himself all primed for the big assault, and then leaps into the fray, and there isn't any resistance at all, it's a hell of a feeling. And there is then, one disappointed revolutionary wandering around, trying to figure out what he was in training for.

That's what happened to Elizabeth Taylor. She revolted, raised the biggest stink she could, and the winds of time blew all the stink away before she'd even got started.

For a few months she wandered around, a revolutionary who'd won her revolt too easily.

And then, on March 26, 1959, in Temple Israel in Hollywood, California, with Rabbi Max Nussbaum officiating, Elizabeth Taylor renounced her Christian Science upbringing and converted to Judaism.

Naturally enough, this conversion was looked on with general skepticism. It looked an awful lot like phase two of the revolution; Elizabeth Taylor acting up again.

If so, phase two worked out a lot better than phase one, at least from the point of view of resistance. Good friends advised her—for her own good—not to make the conversion. After she did anyway, she got a lot of mail from the type of people who hate everybody because God says so. "I wonder why sane people don't write letters any more," she said. "We've heard from everybody but Governor Long."

She had her own explanation for the conversion, claiming it had nothing to do with the revolution, and that she was certainly not cynical enough to use religion as a publicity gimmick.

"When Mike was killed," she said, "a rabbi, Dr. Max Nussbaum of Temple Israel in Hollywood, came to see me.

He talked to me, and all I could ask was, 'Why?' He tried to answer, but he couldn't—and I resented it. He couldn't help the pain in my heart. Then, as the pain lessened, I felt that I wanted to find out the answer for myself. I didn't want to be told. I went back to see Dr. Nussbaum. He gave me a lot of books to read—the philosophy of Judaism, the meaning of Judaism, excerpts from the Bible, the history of the Jews, even the best-seller novel *Exodus*. In seven months, I knew that I had found what I had been searching for for many years."

And, one more point: "Neither Mike Todd nor Eddie Fisher did anything to urge me to become a Jew."

Nevertheless, there is no denying that her religious feelings have always been influenced by the people around her. Short though her marriage was with Nick Hilton, she came out of it interested in the teachings of the Roman Catholic Church. Nick was Roman Catholic, and she started studying Catholic doctrine, then decided that it was too rigid and restrictive for her. But throughout her marriage to Michael Wilding, her religious convictions—shaky and ephemeral as they were—were a strange blend of the Christian Science she had been brought up with and the Roman Catholicism she had met so briefly with Nick Hilton.

There is one more point to be made: At this time, the latter part of 1958 and the early months of 1959, Elizabeth Taylor was more alone than she had ever been in her life. The man she had loved and grown desperately to need was dead. She did not yet have the abiding concern for, and interest in, her children that lights her today. Through her revolt at the time of the Eddie-Debbie fiasco, she had lost even the dubious comradeship of the fans and the gossip columnists.

Alone, completely alone, incredibly alone. She could, had she so desired, have returned to her mother or to Toyland—either would have gladly taken her in. But then the whole purpose of the revolution would have been lost.

She had to be self-sufficient. She had to make her own decisions. She had to learn how to stand on her own two feet.

As she was growing up in Toyland, she had seen one group of men who were constantly making decisions and standing on their own two feet. In fact, they had made most of *her* decisions. They were the studio executives and the film directors. Among them: Louis B. Mayer, Benny Thau, Sam Marx, Lawrence Weingarten, Pandro Berman, Jules Goldstone (her agent), Ben Goetz, and so on and so on and so on.

Conclusion: Judaism promotes self-confidence, the ability to make sure, quick decisions.

Any religion which actively seeks converts—the various Christian sects principally—tells its followers, "Obey the precepts of your religion. Your good example may convert the nonbeliever."

The only reason for changing one's religion is the discovery that the new one fills a need unsatisfied by the old. Elizabeth Taylor's primary need in the fall of 1958, through the winter and spring of 1959, was for self-confidence and self-reliance. All of her life everyone had loved her and fussed over her, and now suddenly she was ostracized. She had to learn to depend on herself, and she had to learn it quickly.

As was stated once before, easy psychological judgments based on hearsay have a habit of being wrong. Elizabeth Taylor's religious motivations are her own business. There is no doubt at all of the depth and sincerity of her religious feelings. The personal motivations that directed these feelings toward Judaism are surely many and complex, as they are in anyone who chooses his religion by any method other than the accident of birth.

"Today, I perform all the rituals and go to a Reform Jewish temple, and I feel as if I have been a Jew all my life."

21

A MONTH AND A HALF LATER she married Eddie Fisher. Elizabeth Taylor has been wedded four times, and no two of the ceremonies were at all alike. Wedding number one was a Spectacular—a combination of the pageantry of Rome and the pageantry of Toyland, 'neath the sunny California skies. Wedding number two was half a world away, neath the cloudy skies of England, and was a semi-private affair—a scant fourteen witnesses to a pageantless civil ceremony at the Caxton Hall registry office, while three thousand oglers milled around outside. Wedding number three was a coronation, a festival, a spur-of-the-moment mardi gras, with the Mayor of Acapulco officiating and the city of Acapulco attending.

Wedding number three out-spectaculared wedding number one. Wedding number four, in an odd example of reality showing for a moment the symmetry of art, out-simpled wedding number two. It took place in Las Vegas, an odd locale for a quiet wedding. It was another religious ceremony, like number one, but there the similarity between them ended. The ceremony this time was Jewish, at Temple Beth Sholom, with a quiet and dignity unique in her weddings. The date was May 12, 1959.

It is not in the ceremonies alone that Elizabeth Taylor's marriages have lacked any discernible pattern. Each marriage has been a completely different situation, lived in different surroundings, faced with different problems, drawing different responses from her friends, her bosses and her public, and involving totally different men.

#1. She was a child bride, a giddy teenager adored by fans scarcely younger than herself. Nick Hilton was a playboy, no more mature than she, and neither were ready or willing to settle into marriage. Their life together was spent, for the most part, in European gambling casinos, except for a month or two in a rented house in California. Communication between them was nil.

#2. Still a child bride, she was now additionally sadder but wiser, a bird with a broken wing. Michael Wilding was urbane, self-satisfied, somewhat irresponsible, and he hid a great deal of sentimentality beneath a sort of yachting-cap sophistication. Their life together was spent, for the most part, in California, in one of two houses, both of which they bought and neither of which they could afford. Their relationship was that of a working family; sharing a common occupation and a common employer. The family included two children, who did not—as one might have predicted—end Elizabeth Taylor's fascination for animals. The marriage lasted nearly five years. Communication between husband and wife was basically one-sided; he expounding and she absorbing; he commanding and she obeying. Communication faltered as she moved inexorably toward an understanding of the possibility of independence.

#3. She was a woman, good and beautiful, ready for emancipation. He was Pegasus, servant to the goddess, but older and more experienced than the goddess. Their life together was one long flight; away from all care and all responsibility. The children were left behind to be cared for by hired hands. Her vocation was left behind, as she lived over a year without stepping in front of a motion picture camera. He showed her reality, her first view of it—but he showed it from above. Communication was intense; they were selling *themselves* to one another, more in being and in movement than in words. They were just returning to the mortal plane when they were parted by his death.

#4. She was alone. Toyland was a crumbled wreckage in the irretrievable past. Her public image was besmirched. She had toughened, too fast. He was a guy who had zoomed into the big time, was somewhat bewildered by it, had let it go to his head, but he was willing to be himself now, but he wasn't sure he remembered who he was. Their life together so far has been a hurried, serious, sometimes belligerent laying down of boundary markers, defining who they are and what they can be. Communication has apparently been clear and complete and two-way; but they are like lost children in the nighttime woods—they can find each other, but they are both still lost.

"Of course, it hasn't been all smooth sailing. We had the typical problems of any young newlyweds, like getting seven thousand letters a week threatening us, like receiving voodoo dolls and communications from different chapters of the Ku

Klux Klan. Worse than that, Hedda Hopper said she wasn't going to write about us any more."

So said Eddie Fisher six months after his marriage to Elizabeth Taylor. From the bubbly unassuming Coca-Cola boy who had relied on the direction and advice of others, he had, in a very short time, grown incredibly tough and independent.

The first three times she married, Elizabeth Taylor had a lot to say about herself, her husband and her marriage. This time she is letting the husband do most of the talking. And he isn't doing badly at it:

"I think I'm nice, I think Elizabeth's nice, and I think people who make mistakes can still be nice."

In the winter of 1958 and the spring of 1959, there were a lot of people who were baffled by the pairing of Eddie Fisher and Elizabeth Taylor. Why he should want to marry her they understood; why she should want to marry him was the baffling part.

Of course, this was because Eddie Fisher was being compared with Mike Todd, and there just wasn't any comparison. The two were incredibly different from one another; Fisher had absolutely none of Todd's self-assurance, years of television work had failed to give him any sort of forceful presence, and he was practically as young as she.

It would have been just as sensible to compare Michael Wilding with Nick Hilton, or Mike Todd with Michael Wilding. It would probably be accurate to say that, in all important respects, four totally different Elizabeth Taylors have married these four totally different men. It would be impossible for her to fluctuate between such pendulum extremes of triumph and tragedy without undergoing far-reaching personality upheavals.

The Elizabeth Taylor who married Eddie Fisher wouldn't have lived the life with Mike Todd that the earlier Elizabeth Taylor had lived. This more recent version is much more aware, for instance, of her responsibilities as a mother; she couldn't travel without her children for months at a time without getting very nervous and upset. She is much more serious about her vocation as an actress than were any of the previous Elizabeth Taylors, and it shows in the kind of work she is doing. It is probably significant that this is the first time in her life that her permanent home is not in California—it is near New York City.

But change is a two-edged sword. Eddie Fisher has also changed. The difference is that he did not marry Elizabeth Taylor as a result of the change. He changed as a result of the marriage. Some of her new toughness and self-reliance rubbed off on him, and the knowledge that they had weathered the storm and were still big time gave him a confidence he had never known before. He has so much confidence now that he can even talk about the lie he used to live:

"Debbie and I were unhappy from the start. We were cast as America's sweethearts in the minds of a great many people and nobody wanted to believe otherwise. We were going to break up a couple of times and I only stayed the last time because Debbie was going to have a baby."

To which Elizabeth Taylor added dryly, "I've never been America's sweetheart, so I never had Eddie's problem."

"I'm just a guy whose marriage was at an end," said Fisher. "I knew it, Debbie knew it, our friends knew it. The public didn't know it. Debbie's studio wouldn't admit it. So I was happily married, as far as the public was concerned, long after I was unhappily married."

Self-confidence and a new toughness haven't been Eddie Fisher's only gains from this, his second marriage. He has also gained in common sense: "If I had to do it all over again, I would, though I think I'd do it more discreetly."

With her personal life returned to something approaching stability, Elizabeth Taylor went back to work. She didn't need the money—she was still half-owner of Michael Todd Co., Inc.—and no one was really sure what sort of reception a movie of hers would get from the general public.

The film was *Suddenly, Last Summer,* in which she was starred with Katherine Hepburn and with her old friend, Montgomery Clift. After its completion, the film's director, Joseph Mankiewicz, said, "She is close to being the greatest actress in the world, and so far she has done it mostly by instinct. She is still a primitive, sort of the Grandma Moses school of acting."

And the writer of the movie, Tennessee Williams, called her, "probably the finest raw talent on the Hollywood screen." As to the specific point, her job in *Suddenly, Last Summer,* he said that, "if nothing else, it demonstrated her ability to rise above miscasting." And, as to why she was back at work again, "I'm inclined to believe that she is more interested in the creative work than the loot."

She received an Academy Award nomination for her role in *Suddenly, Last Summer.* The most recent picture she'd done before that was *Cat on a Hot Tin Roof,* and she'd received an Academy Award nomination for that one, too. And the most recent picture she'd done before *Cat* was *Raintree County,* and she'd received an Academy Award nomination for *that* one, too.

Three motion pictures in a row, all of them made during strained circumstances, and she got best-actress nominations for all three.

Elizabeth Taylor had come a long way from Lassie movies and featherweight comedies. She had come a long way from the mother-dominated child star and the protected fairy princess of Toyland.

Of course, no one can go on and on indefinitely being nominated for Academy Awards. Sooner or later, there has to be a breather picture in which the role is not demanding enough to evoke a performance of Academy Award caliber. The breather picture for Elizabeth Taylor was *BUtterfield 8,* which would complete her contractual obligations with MGM. But her performance in this film is so brilliant and spectacular that once again Elizabeth Taylor has been nominated for an Academy Award.

And then came *Cleopatra.*

22

AMONG INSURANCE UNDERWRITERS, Elizabeth Taylor is considered the worst insurance risk of any movie star, by a long shot. Her illnesses cost the insurance company $45,299 during the shooting of *Raintree County*, and about $75,000 in combined payments for delays caused by her illnesses during *Giant* and *Cat on a Hot Tin Roof*.

Recent years have seen no change in this pattern. Six months after she married Eddie Fisher, she was admitted to the Harkness Pavilion, Columbia Presbyterian Medical Center in New York, with double pneumonia. She was in the hospital from November 26th to December 13th of 1959.

Three months later, March 8, 1960, the Fishers were in Philadelphia, visiting Eddie Fisher's mother. Coming out of a restaurant, Elizabeth Taylor slipped on a patch of ice, fell, and injured her leg. After a preliminary examination at Philadelphia's Nazareth Hospital, she went back to New York, back to the Harkness Pavilion, for further examination and X-rays.

When, in the summer of 1960, she moved to England to begin work on *Cleopatra,* a film for which she was to receive one million dollars, the insurance company looked at her with cautious distrust and charged Twentieth Century-Fox a premium of $390,000 for delay insurance on the film. The $390,000 turned out to be a drop in the bucket.

Filming was supposed to start on September 20th. It didn't. Cast and crew were waiting; rent was being paid on studio space all over London; a fantastically huge and complex set—something like an Egyptian Disneyland—had been constructed outside the city. But Elizabeth Taylor wasn't working.

The only thing anyone knew for sure was that she had last been seen at a costume fitting, at which time it had been discovered by the wardrobe department that the costumes made to her measurements of a few months earlier were now too small for her.

On October 11, 1960, the London *Daily Mail* put two and two together, got the binomial theorem, and published an article stating flatly that the filming of *Cleopatra* was being delayed because Elizabeth Taylor was "too plump" to play the part.

The next thing the *Daily Mail* knew, she slapped them with a lawsuit. This was the first example of Elizabeth Taylor's new policy of public belligerence. A month and a half later, on December 1st, she—and Eddie Fisher—sued half a dozen fan magazines for over seven million dollars, for libel. These latter suits have not as yet been settled, but the suit against the *Daily Mail* was settled on February 14, 1961. The *Daily Mail* settled out of court, with a public apology to Miss Taylor.

Accepting the settlement, her lawyer said that the article that had caused all the ruckus "was particularly distressing since at the time Miss Taylor was seriously ill, which had prevented her for the time being from playing her role in the film." The lawyer magnanimously added, "The fact of Miss Taylor's illness was not known to the defendants at the time when the offending article appeared."

Nor was it known to anyone else. There were rumors of all sorts, but in the fall of 1960 there were no facts. She was seen to enter or leave a hospital every once in a while, but no one seemed to know precisely why, though some headline writers made some rather wild guesses, such as this gem: LIZ STRICKEN WITH RARE FEVER—RUSHED TO HOSPITAL.

Spyros Skouras, the President of Twentieth Century-Fox, and Darryl Zanuck, the company's chief stockholder, had come simultaneously to London at one point to confer with Elizabeth Taylor and with the producer, Walter Wanger. *Cleopatra* was, after all, a twelve-million-dollar film, but even twelve million dollars can't last forever. And Lloyd's, the insurance company involved, was looking at its $390,000 premium and seeing something smaller and smaller every time.

Then, on November 13th, it broke. Screaming with pain, Elizabeth Taylor was carried from her suite at the Dorchester Hotel to a hastily summoned ambulance, and whisked away to the London Clinic. A reporter stated he had heard her say, shakily, her teeth chattering, "Maybe now people will believe I'm *really* sick—and not blame everything on me."

The next day, a platoon of doctors began an extensive examination of Elizabeth Taylor in an effort to diagnose the cause of her violent headaches, fever, and vomiting. Among this covey of physicians was a personal physician to Queen Elizabeth, Lord Evans. In addition, Elizabeth Taylor's personal physician, Dr. Rexford Kennemar, was flying over from the States.

On November 16th, the doctors announced their findings; Elizabeth Taylor was suffering from meningism, complicated by abscessed teeth. A spokesman for one of the doctors, Dr. Carl Goldman, said, "Meningism is more frequently encountered in children than in adults and is of no consequence."

The next day she was out of the hospital again. On November 18th, Walter Wanger announced that *Cleopatra* was being "postponed." On November 19th, it was announced that Elizabeth Taylor was going to California with her husband to recuperate from her recent illness, and would be back in ten days to two weeks.

On December 2nd, she headed back for London, pausing at the New York airport to tell the hovering reporters that she felt fine.

Nobody knew then that that was only round one.

Three months later Elizabeth Taylor suffered her most serious illness—a virulent attack of pneumonia with complications—and, while the world waited with bated breath, fought valiantly for her life.

"The prognosis is not good," said Richard Hanley, Elizabeth Taylor's secretary, on the afternoon of March 4th. Elizabeth had been still alive when she reached the hospital after being rushed there from the Dorchester Hotel, but no one would venture to say how long she could last.

The tracheotomy which the doctors decided to perform in a desperate attempt to save her life was successful but her condition remained grave. In fact, continued breathing difficulties made it necessary to place her in a respirator.

The next day she was still alive, but the regular-style oxygen tent wasn't working properly with her. A Barnet Ventilator, a brand-new electronic respirator in use less than a year in English hospitals, was rushed to the Clinic, and Elizabeth started getting air again.

That was Sunday, the 5th. Monday, she had developed anemia, and the pneumonia had spread to her left lung. She lay motionless in the hospital bed, barely conscious, surrounded by an array of medical machinery to which she was attached by tubes and nodes. She was, because of the anemia, receiving constant blood transfusions. She was being fed intravenously through her ankle. The tube was still in her throat, other tubes were in her nostrils. Well-wishers' flowers had been removed from the room—the doctors were afraid the pollen might affect her breathing. She was in constant pain, but they gave her no sedation; she had to stay conscious in order to keep on breathing.

Four drugs were being fed to her at four-hour intervals with little or no effect. The physicians were afraid she had built up a resistance to them when they had been administered to her in December of 1959, the last time she had fallen ill with pneumonia. In New York, Milton Blackstone, Eddie Fisher's agent, boarded a London-bound plane at Idlewild, carrying a new medicine—staphylococcal bacteriophage lysate.

By Tuesday, the congestion in her lungs had started to clear and touches of color were returning to her face. She was still unable to talk, but she scribbled a note to her husband, Eddie Fisher. It was brief and poignant:

"I love you."

Wednesday, the doctors removed the electronic lung for a while. Gradually, the rest of the week, they lengthened the time she breathed without its help. On Sunday, the 12th, the tube came out of her windpipe.

On the 14th, ten days after it had started, Elizabeth had recovered to the point where her husband could begin to make positive statements about her future. His first one was blunt:

"Elizabeth is not going to do *Cleopatra* in England."

He explained why not: "She thrives on sun and she must have it. That means no more work in England or New York, or any place else where the weather gets bad."

"I appreciate," he said, "what Skouras said—'No Liz, no *Cleopatra'*—but without good weather it will be no Liz. Recently, Liz has made films for the creative excitement she gets from them. Instead of making one or even two films a year, she'll now make one once in a great while."

The next day, Twentieth Century-Fox gave its answer. *Cleopatra* would be filmed in Italy or Egypt or Hollywood. The huge set outside London was to be abandoned. To play the most beautiful woman in the world, you need the most beautiful woman in the world for the role.

Two and a half years before, everybody had hated Liz. People regarded her as a home wrecker, an egotist, a spoiled brat and a hypochondriac. But life is change, and people don't stay mad. Not at the most beautiful woman in the world—who has just gone through hell, again.

On Friday, March 24, 1961, she made her first public statement since her illness:

"I didn't know there was so much love in the world."

On Monday, March 27th, she and her husband took a plane for Los Angeles and the sun.

The End

About the Author

John B. Allan is a well-known article writer whose work has appeared in the nation's leading magazines. He was born in Chicago, attended the University of Chicago and soon afterward began devoting his energies to freelance writing. He served with the Army in World War II and was a legman and special assistant to a prominent writer on Hollywood subjects and people.

Also on Blackbird . . .

THE CASE OF JENNIE BRICE

by

Mary Roberts Rinehart

AND

Hart Island

a novel by

Seth Edgarde

Lightning Source UK Ltd.
Milton Keynes UK
UKOW06f1149071215

264264UK00001B/18/P

9 781610 530323